T0057428

Your
SELF-
DISCOVERY
Journal

A Guided Journey to
Identify and Actualize Your
Passions, Purpose, and Whole Self

Sara Katherine

ADAMS MEDIA
New York London Toronto Sydney New Delhi

Adams Media
An Imprint of Simon & Schuster, Inc.
100 Technology Center Drive
Stoughton, Massachusetts 02072

First Adams Media hardcover edition December 2021

ADAMS MEDIA and colophon are trademarks of Simon & Schuster.

For information about special discounts for bulk purchases, please contact Simon & Schuster Special Sales at 1-866-506-1949 or business@simonandschuster.com.

The Simon & Schuster Speakers Bureau can bring authors to your live event. For more information or to book an event contact the Simon & Schuster Speakers Bureau at 1-866-248-3049 or visit our website at www.simonspeakers.com.

Interior design, illustrations, and hand lettering by Priscilla Yuen

Manufactured in the United States of America

2 2022

ISBN 978-1-5072-1729-0

To Geordi, my wonderful family, and all of my supportive friends who have helped me through my own self-discovery journey every step of the way.

CONTENTS

PART 4 DISCOVER YOUR MOTIVATIONS.. 113

PART 5 DISCOVER HOW YOU CONNECT WITH OTHERS............... 145

INTRODUCTION

“ Have you been craving more out of life but
aren't sure exactly what you want? ”

“ Or maybe you know what you want but don't know
where to start? ”

“ Do you feel as though you've been traveling
along a path that isn't right for you? ”

If you answered yes to any of these questions, you're in the
right place! In order to figure out how to feel more content with
your life, you need to start with the basics—who you are. You need
to understand what is important to you, what makes you feel more
fulfilled, and also what you need from your relationships with others.
This is where self-discovery comes in. Self-discovery is the ultimate
secret for overall personal growth. After all, you can't expect to start
cultivating a happier, healthier life when you don't know what that
would look like for your unique self.

Your Self-Discovery Journal will enable you to answer the
question of who you are through interactive journal prompts you can
complete in the following pages as well as activities you can apply
in your daily life. Self-discovery involves both introspective and

extrinsic work, and this balance of prompts and activities will allow you to reap the benefits of both. Even something as simple as trying one activity per day can take you a long way toward uncovering key things about yourself and what you want in life. You'll move through sections organized to help you learn more about your personality and values, then cultivate self-love and confidence, determine your purpose and passions in life, understand your motivations, and identify how you connect with other people. To gain everything the journey of self-discovery has to offer, you will want to work through each section consecutively, though certain activities in each section may feel more impactful or relevant than others, depending on your own experiences.

You'll:

- ✔ Get a new perspective on your life
- ✔ Distinguish your strengths
- ✔ Create a bucket list
- ✔ Set SMART (specific, measurable, attainable, relevant, and time-based) goals
- ✔ Examine your role models
- ✔ And much more!

This book is your personal guide for connecting on a deeper level with who you are and for recognizing what it is you need in order to live an authentically aligned life for *you*. Throughout each activity, trust your intuition and follow whatever sparks your interest. You never know what you'll find out about yourself along the way. Your path to self-discovery begins now!

SELF-DISCOVERY 101

“ What *is* self-discovery? **”**

The basic definition is to discover more about yourself, which sounds simple enough, but when you dive deeper, a lot lies beneath this surface understanding. At its core, self-discovery is the all-encompassing journey of personal growth. Beyond learning your personality type and finding your "dream" career, it involves digging deep to truly understand who you are, what you want, and what makes you tick. It's about your values, your thoughts and feelings, your hope for the future, and so much more. If you're feeling stuck, struggling to make decisions for yourself, wishing for more confidence, or ultimately feeling lost in life, self-discovery is the key to kick-starting the reality you want and attaining your goals. In Part 1, you'll examine self-discovery in more detail, from why it matters to what the path toward self-discovery looks like.

Why Is Self-Discovery Important?

Self-discovery is truly where you need to start when you're ready to grow and change your life. Why? Because if you don't connect with the core of who you are, you'll find yourself simply following what other people or society expects from you. Unsure of what you want and need, you'll start stumbling down a path that ultimately may not feel right for you, just because it's one you've seen others take.

That's the complete opposite of what you want when you start your personal development journey.

When you connect with your inner self and truly understand your values, what you want in life, your passions, and what you need in your relationships with other people, you'll feel more confident in your decisions and move toward a path that feels more authentically aligned with you. That means that you'll finally be able to assuredly make decisions for yourself without caring about what other people think. You'll know how to set healthy boundaries with other people that help protect your values and improve your relationships. Ultimately, you'll take strides toward putting yourself first. This is where the magic happens and where you'll truly change your life for the better.

What to Expect During Your Self-Discovery Journey

This book is going to help you navigate through the five main facets for your self-discovery and personal growth journey, providing both reflective journal prompts and action-based activities to take into your day-to-day life. The biggest goal for you is both to do the inner work and to take action. Many people get stuck in the learning phase of personal growth and self-discovery, forgetting to actually take what they've learned from the books they read and apply it to their lives. This happens in part due to fear of change or the unknown or simply not knowing how to apply what they've learned to their lives. This book was created to give you clear, actionable steps to move past the learning phase and fully apply the knowledge you gain to help you grow.

The five main parts of self-discovery that you will explore in detail throughout this book are as follows.

1 Discover Your Inner Self

Become familiar with everything that makes you, you! This is the core foundation to help you along your self-discovery journey. Why? Because everything in your life—from your goals to your relationships with others and yourself—is impacted by how you think, feel, and believe deep in your heart. If you don't understand exactly who you are and what you want in your life at the core, you won't be able to move forward with other areas of personal development. For example, if you want to work on your confidence or on setting healthy boundaries with others, you first have to understand what makes you amazing or what you need from a relationship in order to be satisfied. What goals will you set if you don't know what you want, what your strengths are, or what you value?

Through the Part 1 activities, you will examine your inner self in more depth. What you uncover here will be the building blocks for the rest of the themes you will explore throughout this book. Some examples of activities in Part 1 include identifying your values, exploring personality tests, and visualizing your biggest dreams. It's time to kick off your self-discovery journey!

2 Discover Self-Love

Once you've discovered more about your inner self, you'll be ready for the next step: building up your confidence and becoming your own biggest fan! A big part of your self-discovery journey will be growing to love everything about yourself as you get to know who you are. This even means recognizing your insecurities and reshaping your mindset to appreciate the things you may have deemed flaws in the past. You will start this step of your journey in Part 2.

Of course, the activities in this section aren't going to completely eliminate your self-doubt or insecurities. There will always be situations in life that encourage these feelings. Instead, you will work on creating a strong foundation of confidence. Confidence is a muscle. We're all born with some level of it; it's up to you to train and strengthen your own confidence over time. The stronger it is, the more self-assured you'll feel on a regular basis, even in those low moments.

3 Discover Your Purpose and Passions

Once you've built foundations for both basic self-discovery and self-love, it will be time to dive deep into discovering your purpose and passions in life. What's the difference between the two? In the simplest terms, passions are things you absolutely love to do. These are all of the activities that you're constantly pulled to and enjoy doing on a regular basis. A purpose, on the other hand, is how you feel you best contribute to the world. Purpose is a much more focused version of passion, because it's still something you enjoy doing, but it has a clear direction toward benefiting someone or something other than yourself. For example, you may have a passion for music. This can manifest as writing music, playing an instrument, or experiencing your favorite artists in concert. When it comes to your purpose, this could be something like using the music you write to change the lives of others. You have a message or a reason behind your music that extends beyond something you enjoy.

One important key to keep in mind about finding purpose is that it doesn't have to be one single thing. Many people pressure themselves to know what their "ultimate purpose" is, but your discovery doesn't have to be a big, intimidating task. In fact, you may find multiple purposes as you grow and change throughout your life! The activities in Part 3 will help you explore different avenues for both finding your purpose and discovering your passions. Identifying either of these throughout your life will help you reconnect with yourself and help you enjoy a more fulfilled and authentic life overall.

4 Discover Your Motivations

What drives you to keep striving for your work and personal goals, even when things get overwhelming or honestly just boring? There are so many different ways you can find motivation, increase productivity, and manage your time. And with so much to balance in life—relationships, career aspirations, everyday responsibilities, and more—having a solid understanding of what works best for you in staying motivated along the way is going to help build a robust tool belt for accomplishing all of your biggest goals!

The activities in Part 4 will help you better understand how to encourage your ambition, increase your productivity, and manage your time. Everyone is different when it comes to managing their daily lives or finding exactly what motivates them. Some people find that playing upbeat music gets them motivated. Others prefer listening to podcasts as they work to stay focused throughout the day. In this section, you will discover what feels right for you.

5 Discover How You Connect with Others

The last step along your journey to self-discovery is understanding how you connect with other people and manage the relationships in your life. This includes your connections with friends, family members, coworkers, classmates, teammates—anyone you have a relationship with. It's important to know how you interact with others and how to best navigate the different relationships in your life in the healthiest ways possible. Understanding your relationships with other people helps you recognize when you need to set new or stronger boundaries, allows you to empathize better, and helps you develop a deeper appreciation for all of the incredible supporters you have in your inner circle.

In Part 5, you'll dive into how to understand the interpersonal behaviors and needs of yourself and those you know, resolve conflicts, stop harmful people-pleasing habits, and so much more.

Tips for Your Journey

As you work through each section in this book, keep an open mind and heart. You may learn some things about yourself that make you uncomfortable or afraid, but that's part of the journey. We all have to recognize both the good and the uncomfortable within ourselves and our lives in order to create a life that's authentically aligned with our unique goals and dreams. If you do start to feel a bit uncertain about what you're learning about yourself, feel free to take a step back and think about the reasons behind your emotions. Is there a different way to look at what you're thinking? For example, if you learn that you need healthier boundaries with other people in your life, you may become uncomfortable with the fact that you've given of yourself to too many people who take advantage of your kindness. Hold space to feel your emotions, and then take note of ways that you can gently approach setting and enforcing the boundaries that you need to create to build these healthier relationships in your life.

How will you know you've made progress along your journey? Notice how you feel, especially when it comes to your overall confidence and the clarity you have about your goals. You'll start noticing what feels good and what doesn't fit you when someone asks you questions about your future. You'll start trusting your intuition when making decisions rather than asking other people for their opinions. The change will be subtle, but check in with yourself over time and see if you notice some of these small shifts that develop within yourself through your self-discovery journey.

You've already taken such an incredible, beautiful step forward by picking up this book and choosing to explore it. However you use it—whether you do the activities in each part in order or bounce around to those that stand out; try one or more activities every day or flip through more occasionally when the need strikes—any small step is going to propel you toward changing your life for the better. All that's left to do is to turn the page and get started!

PART 1

DISCOVER
YOUR
Inner Self

LEARN YOUR MYERS-BRIGGS PERSONALITY TYPE

Personality tests are an excellent way to begin getting to know yourself better. The Myers-Briggs Type Indicator is one of the most popular free personality tests available online. This assessment allows you to reflect on how you perceive the world and make decisions. It then assigns you to one of each of the four categories: Introversion or Extraversion (whether you tend to focus more on your inner world or the external world around you); Sensing or Intuition (whether you tend to focus on the reality of a situation or the possibilities); Thinking or Feeling (whether you tend to make decisions based on logical reasoning or personal values and feelings); and Judging or Perceiving (whether you prefer schedules and clear boundaries and deadlines or prefer that things be more open-ended).

Go to www.16personalities.com and take the personality test to discover your Myers-Briggs personality type. When reviewing your results, notice if any specific scenarios or descriptions you read help you better understand who you are, your strengths and weaknesses, how your personality fits with certain career paths, how you behave within romantic relationships and friendships, and even how you prefer to approach parenthood. The Myers-Briggs test results are incredibly detailed, so keep your personality type in mind as you start diving into your self-discovery journey! Also realize that some people notice that their Myers-Briggs results change as they continue to learn and grow throughout life, so make sure to go back and take the test every once in a while to see if you've evolved in any way.

DISCOVER YOUR ENNEAGRAM NUMBER

Another fantastic personality test to take for self-discovery is the Enneagram Personality Test. This test is based on the Enneagram personality theory, which states that personalities are derived from nine different types, represented by the numbers 1–9. Each type, or number, is driven by their own core emotions, values, and fears, which in turn drive their response to the world around them. Something unique about Enneagram is that the theory states that everyone has a little bit of each number within themselves. However, at the end of the day, you will always have one core number that fits you best. And unlike with Myers-Briggs, your Enneagram type doesn't change over time. You might bring in traits from other numbers in certain situations, like if you're stressed or confident, but you will still have the same dominant number.

Go to www.eclecticenergies.com/enneagram/test and take the free assessment to discover your Enneagram number. Once you have determined your number and read your results, do a bit more research to learn more about what that number can mean for your life. A great book to read to learn more about your Enneagram personality type is *The Enneagram & You: Understand Your Personality Type and How It Can Transform Your Relationships* by Gina Gomez (Adams Media, 2020). As you discover more about your type, you'll learn about your strengths, your weaknesses, and how you relate to other people, all of which create a great foundation for the beginning of your self-discovery journey.

IDENTIFY YOUR VALUES

One of the most important keys to truly understanding yourself is identifying what you value. Why is this so important? Your values are the foundation of how you go about your life. These are the core beliefs that you feel most aligned with. They help you navigate decisions, goals, and relationships with a clear sense of what is right for you. That feeling in your gut when you intuit that something is wrong? You're likely experiencing a situation where your values are being compromised.

On the following lines, write down at least three values that you resonate with the most. What are three things that you absolutely cannot compromise on? If you're having trouble, some examples include:

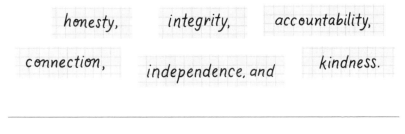

honesty, integrity, accountability,

connection, independence, and kindness.

_____

_____

_____

Whenever you're having a hard time making a decision, refer back to your values to better align with the choice that's most authentic for you.

SURPASS YOUR COMFORT ZONE

When you find yourself regularly feeling stuck and unmotivated, you've likely allowed yourself to live within the cozy space of your comfort zone for far too long. Your comfort zone is filled with everything that's easy and familiar to you. It's a great place! But if you stay there for too long, it becomes difficult to learn new things and grow as a person. If you've been feeling stuck in a rut lately, stepping outside of your comfort zone can give you that push you need to get out of it.

Easier said than done? Of course! Why do you think people prefer to stay in their comfort zone? It's warm and familiar and not filled with all of the uncertainties that live beyond this space. But what else is included in the unfamiliar?

DISCOVERY **GROWTH**

Endless Possibilities

Try one thing this week that's outside of your comfort zone. Strike up a conversation with someone new, take a class to learn a new skill, or simply try something from this book! It doesn't have to be anything huge—just one task that makes you a little bit scared. Feel the fear, and do it anyway. You never know what you'll discover about yourself along the way!

STOP SEEKING PERFECTION

Perfection may feel like an attractive standard to uphold for yourself, but sometimes focusing on being "perfect" holds you back from being your authentic self. In reality, there is no such thing as perfect. No single person on this earth is perfect, no matter how much they may look like they are in photos on *Instagram* or through the achievements they share online.

If you're holding back because you're always trying to be perfect, whether it's at work, in your presence online, in your relationships, or anywhere else, you're likely wasting precious energy and time. Next time you work on a project or get caught up in the idea of being "perfect," recite this mantra:

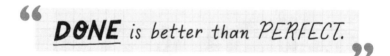

" **DONE** is better than *PERFECT.* "

Finish your task to the best of your ability, and know that you tried the best you could. Once you start accepting that you've done your best in those moments, you'll be able to learn and grow from these experiences for next time, no matter the result.

BREAK THROUGH LIMITING BELIEFS

Have you ever heard a voice in your head telling you that you can't accomplish something? That you should stay in your comfort zone? Those are limiting beliefs that are holding you back from being able to grow in ways that can get uncomfortable. As you go through your self-discovery journey, you're going to realize new dreams that you want to accomplish, but you'll need to break through your limiting beliefs.

What are some of your biggest dreams?

_____

_____

_____

_____

_____

What are some fears or limiting beliefs that you have
about pursuing those dreams?

_____

_____

_____

_____

_____

_____

Rewrite these fears into reasons why you *can* accomplish those dreams.

In other words, how can some of these fears be used as strengths instead? For example, if you're scared to switch careers because you don't want to feel like you're abandoning your current team, think of this as you having a value of caring for your coworkers and wanting the best for where you are now. You can easily bring this strength into a future job you decide to pursue.

_____

_____

_____

_____

_____

_____

_____

_____

_____

_____

You truly can accomplish anything. Don't let the inner critic in your head hold you back!

VISUALIZE YOUR BIGGEST DREAMS

Visualization is a powerful tool for both discovering and achieving what you want in life. Some of the most successful athletes, entrepreneurs, actors, and CEOs in the world swear by the power of visualization, claiming it as a huge part of their overall success. Jim Carrey, Oprah Winfrey, and Michael Jordan are just a small sample of the many people who recommend visualizing your dreams.

Regularly visualizing yourself achieving your goals not only helps you keep these dreams in the front of your mind every day, but it trains your brain to perform in a way that will help you achieve those goals, seeking out all of the opportunities necessary to get to where you want to be.

Take a moment and think about one of your goals. Take a deep breath and visualize yourself already living your life having achieved this goal. How does it feel? Who are you with? What does it look like? Try to imagine as many details as possible. This may be challenging at first, but set a timer and try 3 minutes of visualization each day. Work your way up to 10 minutes each day, and notice how much more confident you feel about the path you're taking to create your dream life.

DESCRIBE YOURSELF IN ONE WORD

Feeling lost and unsure about who you are? Don't really know where to start if you were to describe yourself? Start with just one word! What is one word that describes who you are? Don't think too hard on this one; go with your gut. It doesn't have to be one word that completely embodies who you are, but something that you think feels right for you. Ask a few friends if you're truly stuck, but start developing trust with your own instincts and opinions with just one word:

_____

What does this word mean to you? How does this make you feel? Are there ways you can embody this word in your daily life more regularly than you have before? Note: If the word that pops into your head initially is more negative (such as *jealous*), give yourself grace and tap in to your intuition a bit more. What is a more positive word that comes to light?

_____

_____

_____

_____

_____

_____

GET A BIRD'S-EYE VIEW

Sometimes when you're stuck trying to figure out how to solve a problem, it's easy to get caught up in your own head. When you're looking at something solely from your point of view, you're more likely to start thinking in circles, unable to solve the problem or make a decision. If you find yourself in this situation, one way to break the endless thought cycle is to ask someone else for their opinion.

Reaching out to a friend or colleague for their point of view can help you view your current issue with a new perspective. Their opinion on the matter likely will help you think of new options and solutions to help you solve your problem or make a decision, leading you to a better understanding of how you will navigate similar predicaments in the future, and what options feel the most aligned for you. However, don't go to just anyone; make sure it's someone you trust and respect. They'll have your best interest in mind and will try to help you come to a solution that feels right for you.

HAVE A CONVERSATION WITH YOURSELF

Talking to yourself probably sounds like a weird suggestion, but it's actually very normal! In fact, it can be healthy and incredibly beneficial, depending on what you're experiencing. Talking to yourself out loud can help you process your thoughts and learn more about yourself in many situations, such as:

- ✔ Preparing for a tough but necessary conversation
- ✔ Practicing for an interview
- ✔ Solving a math problem
- ✔ Outlining your thought habits
- ✔ Calming down anxiety or stress

Above all, having a conversation with yourself out loud helps you get out of your head. It helps your brain slow down, so you can connect everything that's spinning in your mind into words. Try this next time you feel overwhelmed or stuck, especially if you prefer to talk things out rather than writing them down to clear your head. Have a simple conversation as if you were talking to someone else, and don't judge yourself! You're being practical and trying something completely normal. It might feel a bit silly at first, but notice how much better you feel after this conversation!

READ MORE BOOKS

When was the last time you read something new? Not just a new book, but a new genre or author? If you've read a book outside of your usual reading comfort zone, great job! You're already one step ahead. If not, but reading books is a go-to method of personal growth, you're still amazing! But let's take it a step further.

While reading is something that you do in school to learn and grow, it's often put on the back burner after graduation instead of turning into a regular hobby. It's easy to get caught up in the latest *Netflix* show or browse social media to pass the time, but the value of reading new books is priceless. It doesn't have to be nonfiction! No matter what it is, if you're reading something new, you can discover something new about yourself, such as new genres, writing styles, or authors that you like.

Next time you are in a bookstore or are browsing books online, step outside of your comfort zone and take a look at different categories than you usually choose from. If you usually go for mysteries, try your hand at some historical fiction. Love personal development? Try biographies! You never know what you might like until you try it, and you never know what you'll learn about yourself!

DO A LIFE AUDIT

One of the most effective activities you can do to clear your mind and kick-start your self-discovery journey is a "life audit." This is like spring-cleaning for your mind. When you have a lot going on, your mind can get jumbled about what's causing you stress, what you need to prioritize, and so on. Performing a life audit can clean out your thoughts and help you get clear about next steps.

Write down everything that comes to mind about any facet of your life: your friends, family, career, confidence, hobbies, finances—literally anything! Don't judge or hold back. Once finished, look over your audit and pinpoint what areas you need to focus on first as you start your self-discovery journey.

WIN THE LOTTERY

Imagine that one day you hit the jackpot. No, really: You just won $10 million! Now what's next? How are you going to manage the money? The possibilities are endless. Would you prefer to save some before spending the rest on something you've always dreamed of purchasing? Would you share your newfound wealth with family and friends? Would you donate it? Take a trip to your dream destination?

Describe in as much detail as possible what you would do after winning the lottery. You'd be surprised with how much this tells you about the person you are and what you find most important in your life!

_____

_____

_____

_____

_____

_____

_____

_____

_____

_____

_____

_____

TRY A NEW SKILL

Have you ever daydreamed about mastering a new skill? Maybe you've always wondered what it would be like to play the guitar or start a blog. Alternatively, have you seen someone else you admire excel at a skill and wondered what it would be like to do the same? For example, maybe you know someone who is excellent at public speaking. They captivate the crowd and have them hanging on every word.

Thought of your skill? Great! Now get to work.

Take one step today toward honing this skill. Don't second-guess yourself or worry that you won't be any good. Just do it! Learning something new is always going to be a bit rocky to begin with, but you'll never know if it's something you love unless you try.

GIVE YOUR LIFE A 100 PERCENT BOOST

Are you dying for one particular thing to happen in your life? It can be anything—a big dream of yours, an event, a mere stroke of luck. Take some time to really think about this: What is one thing that would make your life 100 percent better if it happened? Most important, *why* would this one thing improve your life so much? Be as detailed as possible.

_____

_____

_____

_____

_____

_____

_____

_____

_____

_____

With this in mind, is there anything about this event that you have control over right now? What's one thing you can do today to get yourself closer to the desired outcome you just described?

_____

_____

_____

_____

REMOVE THE LIMITS

What are some of your biggest dreams? Seriously, if you could do literally anything possible right now, what would it be? Now why haven't you done this already? Is money and/or time an issue that's holding you back? Unfortunately, these are two common roadblocks that many face to accomplish their biggest dreams.

However, what would you do if time and money weren't an issue at all? Imagine that you had an endless amount of money and unlimited time. What would be your biggest dream then? Would things change with this in mind?

REFLECT ON YOUR EVOLUTION

When you're caught up in the regular day-to-day routine, simply trying to make it to the end of the week, it's easy to forget how much you've accomplished and grown over the last one, two, and especially three years.

Reflecting on the past few years helps you realize just how much small steps can make a big impact in your life and personal growth over time. On the days that you feel defeated or like you're not seeing much progress, take some time to think about how far you've come already. Don't discount your hard work!

Think back through the last three years: How much have you changed? How does that past version of you compare to the person you are today?

_____

_____

_____

_____

_____

_____

_____

_____

_____

_____

_____

_____

_____

FIND SOURCES OF STRENGTH

When you're feeling scared or uncertain about something happening in your life, what do you do to find strength? Is there anyone who gives you the courage you need to take on a challenging task? Is there a practice that makes you feel empowered, like working out at the gym or dancing to your favorite upbeat songs? Think about a few times that you've felt fearful about trying something new or taking a risk. Who or what did you pull from as sources of strength? Write down these sources here.

_____

_____

_____

_____

_____

_____

_____

_____

_____

_____

Next time you find yourself facing your fears and need an extra boost in order to move forward, refer to these sources of strength to tap in to the courage you need!

CHASE BIG DREAMS

Think back to when you were little, when one of the most popular questions people asked you was, What do you want to do when you grow up? Sometimes that answer was easy: "A firefighter!" or "A movie star!" But as you grow older, that question carries more weight. Your dreams have conditions, like money, time, and experience.

It's time to throw these conditions to the side and reconnect with some of your wildest ambitions. What are the biggest dreams that you've had for a very long time? Have you put off doing things or visiting places you've always wanted to?

_____

_____

_____

_____

_____

_____

_____

_____

_____

_____

Next to each of these big dreams, write one easy step that you can take to start following these dreams. Don't make any excuses; all it takes is one step at a time.

BRING BACK THE SPARK

When you start getting to know yourself better, there's a big chance that some activities or relationships in your life may feel a bit out of alignment compared to how they used to make you feel. The more you learn about who you are and what you really want, the more you'll want to shift various areas of your life to match the personal growth you're experiencing internally. For example, if you've learned that you value honesty and integrity, but you notice that many of your friends don't uphold these values, these friendships are likely to feel out of alignment for you and the life you want to live in the long run. This can also apply to jobs, hobbies, how you like to spend your free time, and more.

The good news is that hope is not lost! You *can* bring that spark back into your life. Keep an eye open for things that feel good and truly in alignment with the vision for your life that you're uncovering. Trust your instincts and lean into new experiences, even if they're scary. Anytime you find a taste of that spark of joy, grab on to it and see where it takes you!

EXPRESS YOUR CREATIVITY

How do you like to express yourself creatively? Even if you don't consider yourself a naturally creative person, flexing your creative muscle is a great exercise to get out of your head and reconnect with something that feels good for you.

Here are some ideas to help you get started:

These are just a few ways you can express creativity. Try a couple of these options this week and see if you find your creative spark!

PINPOINT YOUR LEARNING STYLE

Have you ever found yourself struggling to retain information when listening to someone lecture or give a speech? Or maybe you really don't effectively understand something new unless you've participated in a hands-on experience? Everyone has their own unique style of learning, and a better understanding of how *you* learn best is a very effective tool to have under your belt.

There are four main learning styles:

1 **VISUAL LEARNING:**
You learn best by seeing visual depictions of information, such as charts, graphics, or symbols.

 2 **AUDITORY LEARNING:**
You learn best by hearing new information, such as by attending lectures or reading aloud to yourself.

 3 **READING/WRITING LEARNING:**
You learn best through writing things down and taking notes, as well as reading text in books or online articles.

 4 **KINESTHETIC LEARNING:**
You learn best by taking a hands-on approach, actively practicing what you're learning in order to truly process new information.

Which type of learning style fits you best? You may identify with more than one, which is completely normal. Incorporating multiple ways that you best process new information can help you learn new things even more effectively.

GET OUT OF YOUR OWN WAY

How many times have you told yourself that you were ready to grow or change a habit in your life, but you didn't want to actually *do* anything different? Here's an example: Let's say your dentist is constantly finding cavities in your teeth, and you *know* you don't brush your teeth every day. The dentist recommends you brush twice a day, and by doing so, you'll decrease your chances of getting more cavities. You go home, try it for a few days, and then think, "Nah, this isn't changing anything." Next thing you know, you're falling back into old habits.

The next time you see your dentist, you have more cavities. Are you shocked? Probably not. The same idea goes for personal growth and self-discovery. If you feel that you need to change and *want* to change, you're going to need to try new things. You're going to need to get uncomfortable. But it's all part of the journey, and it *will* be worth it in the end.

Not sure how to get out of your own way when things get uncomfortable? Here are a few ideas that can help:

- ✔ Find an accountability buddy
- ✔ Schedule your new goals/habits on your calendar
- ✔ Make a contract for yourself and sign it
- ✔ Hire a coach for extra support

All of these options and more will help increase your chance of not allowing old habits to sabotage your progress toward your new goals.

CALM YOUR EGO

Your ego is what helps you interpret reality and your own personal identity. It's what drives you to think in certain ways and have perspectives and opinions about your own experiences. But while it means well, your ego is often misguided, striving to keep you in your comfort zone rather than growing and trying new things. Why? Because trying something new is scary! What if something goes wrong? What if other people make fun of you? Why not just stay in this safe bubble of life that you know well enough already?

On your self-discovery journey, you're going to need to take steps to calm your ego in order to step out of your comfort zone more confidently. Gently encourage it to learn that the risks you're taking are for the best, brightest version of who you want to be. One of the simplest ways to calm your ego when it's flaring with limiting beliefs and fears is to take a step back and give your mind some space. This can be done through meditation, focused breathing, regular mental breaks, and affirmations. Here are some affirmations you can say to yourself when you notice your ego is getting scared:

"My beliefs are under **MY CONTROL.**"

"I am **SAFE** and can **HANDLE** anything life throws at me."

"The risks I take are helping me become the **BEST VERSION** of myself that I can be."

BREAK THROUGH SOCIETAL EXPECTATIONS

Whether you realize it or not, society has a huge impact on your beliefs and the expectations you have for your life. Each generation is impacted by society's current expectations in some way. Expectations also change over the course of decades, as the expectations of a woman's role in the household have. Another example: Most modern college students are expected to graduate with their bachelor's degree in four years, right after high school. But what if you take a gap year, or wait even longer, until you truly feel ready? You're going against society's expectations, which may impose unhappy beliefs that you aren't successful enough or are wasting your time.

What expectations from society are holding you back? Why are these expectations irrelevant to your own journey?

_____

_____

_____

_____

_____

_____

_____

_____

_____

_____

_____

SQUASH THE WORST-CASE SCENARIO

When you're trying something new or taking risks outside of your comfort zone, fear and anxiety will urge you to hold back. Often your mind will present you with all of the worst possible scenarios, encouraging you to do anything possible to avoid experiencing the worst outcome.

If you're experiencing this right now, what is truly the worst thing that can happen? Really sit down and think about it, and describe it in the following space.

_____

_____

_____

_____

_____

If you do experience this worst-case scenario, what will you do to handle it?

_____

_____

_____

_____

_____

You can truly do anything if you put your mind to it. You are *so* incredibly capable of handling even the worst situations that you could imagine!

ENJOY THE JOURNEY

As you explore yourself along this journey of discovery, you're probably already feeling revved up and excited to achieve all of these incredible new goals you've set—which is great! However, keep in mind that there is also beauty in what you're experiencing right now. Even though you may not technically be where you want to be yet, you're still learning and growing in an extraordinary way, and achieving your biggest goals isn't the only thing worth celebrating.

Try your best to not get stuck in a "grass is always greener" outlook as you start setting and working toward new goals. It's easy to get caught in the cycle of achieving a goal and then immediately working toward setting a new one without quite enjoying where you are now. Take some time to express gratitude for your overall journey—all of the highs and lows, even when it's tough. You're on the right track and will end up wherever you're supposed to be. You may as well enjoy it while you're on your way!

LET GO OF REGRETS

Are you someone who holds on to regret? Have you been feeling guilty for a while about something that you're struggling to release? While many times you'll hear that you should live your life without regrets, you'll likely experience guilt for something you did in the past at some point in your life. However, there are ways you can forgive yourself and let these regrets go.

What is one regret you've been holding on to? What is something you've learned from this regretful experience?

_____

_____

_____

_____

_____

_____

_____

_____

_____

_____

_____

At the end of the day, this experience helped you learn something about yourself and how you can approach similar situations in the future. Acknowledge this, and let go of the guilt.

WRITE A LETTER TO YOUR FUTURE SELF

Take some time to think about your ideal future self. Where do you see yourself in one year? Three years? Even five? Keep this vision in your head and take time to write a letter to your future self. What do you want to tell them? What do you want them to remember?

_____

_____

_____

_____

_____

_____

_____

_____

_____

_____

_____

_____

_____

Consider saving this letter in an envelope and labeling it "Do not read until [year]." Make a plan to refer back to it once you've become your future self and reflect on what it said. Also, you can visit www.futureme.org and write a letter that will automatically be emailed to you in as many years as you'd like!

ACKNOWLEDGE YOUR PRESENT SELF

While addressing your younger and future self are fantastic exercises, don't forget about the person that you are today. You are unique, incredible, wonderful, and *so* many other things, right here, right now. Don't forget to acknowledge all of the progress and growth you've made up to this point, even if you're just starting your self-discovery journey!

How did you get to where you are today? Go into as much detail as possible, and reflect back with gratitude!

PART 2

DISCOVER
Self-Love

IDENTIFY YOUR STRENGTHS

When you struggle with loving yourself, it's easy to focus on everything that you don't like about yourself. Thinking negatively breeds even more negative thoughts, and pretty soon you're stuck in a thought pattern that's hard to get out of! Luckily you can move forward and grow past these negative beliefs. Your first step? Identifying your strengths.

What are you good at? What are some of your strongest characteristics, habits, or talents? Write them down.

_____

_____

_____

_____

_____

_____

_____

_____

_____

_____

Anytime you notice that you're viewing yourself in a negative light, refer back to this list and add a few more strengths to remind yourself how amazing you are. Eventually, you'll train your brain to focus on the positives rather than getting stuck on the negatives!

NOTICE YOUR WEAKNESSES

You're probably thinking: "Wait, you just told me not to focus on the negatives. Why would you recommend noticing my weaknesses?" Well, there's a big difference between acknowledging your weaknesses and thinking negatively: judgment. Feeling ashamed about yourself is different from simply being self-aware.

It's tough to truly be aware of who you are if you aren't familiar with the parts of yourself that need a little more attention. Becoming self-aware helps you embrace your imperfections. Above all, weaknesses make you human. Everyone is imperfect; there's no need to feel ashamed of who you are!

Acknowledge a few of your weaknesses. Don't judge yourself; simply recognize them. You're practicing self-awareness, and over time you'll start to embrace your weaknesses along with your strengths.

CELEBRATE YOUR ACCOMPLISHMENTS

When was the last time you celebrated achieving one of your goals? It's so easy to forget to take time to celebrate when you're constantly working on projects, your personal development, fitness milestones, or any other goals. Your automatic reaction is often to start thinking of the next steps, the next goals to work toward in your life. But what happens when you forget to stop and celebrate your accomplishments? You can feel burned out, overwhelmed, and exhausted.

What was the last goal—or even a small win—that you accomplished? Celebrate it today. Take yourself out to your favorite restaurant, watch that new indie film you've been wanting to see, or dance your heart out to your favorite playlist. Do something that makes you smile—you deserve it! And don't stop there. Keep celebrating your accomplishments every step of the way!

EMBRACE WHAT MAKES YOU UNIQUE

There is absolutely no one on this planet who is exactly like you. While it may sound like a cliché, it's 100 percent true! No matter how similar you feel you are to someone else in your life—whether it's a sibling, best friend, or someone else—there will always be something about you that's different from the other person. And you know what? That's incredible to think about.

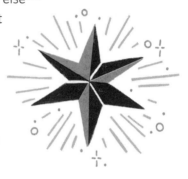

Next time you're feeling down on yourself or struggling with self-love, remind yourself of this fact: You are beautifully, uniquely you. That in itself is something to be proud of.

You will always bring something different to a conversation. You will always have a unique opinion, personality trait, or talent that's not exactly the same as someone else's. Even if something about you seems commonplace, your experiences, emotions, and every part of you combine to make a whole that is unlike anyone else. Hold that thought close to your heart, and give yourself gratitude and love for being your unique, wonderful self.

LIST WHAT YOU'RE PROUD OF

If you're struggling with self-love, particularly self-confidence, you're likely having a hard time feeling proud of yourself. It's easy to forget your accomplishments when your self-esteem is a bit low, but you truly have so much to be proud of, even if you don't realize it yet! For example, you woke up today, right? Did you get out of bed? Even if not, you're reading this book right now and working on yourself—that's fantastic! Even small achievements are worth celebrating. Write some down right now.

LOOK THE PART

Visualize your future self: What do you do? How do you feel? Now get a little more detailed. What are you wearing? How does your outfit make you feel? Now come back to the present day. What do you wear on a regular basis? Does this match the visualization you just had in your head? If not, for a few days this week, dress like this visualized ideal of yourself. Whether that's dressing up or wearing comfortable clothes you love, you'd be surprised how much what you wear each day can have an impact on how you feel overall. Wearing clothes that not only look good to you but also help you *feel* good can do wonders for your self-confidence and ability to think lovingly of yourself.

When you try it out this week, be aware of how you feel while wearing these types of clothes. If you notice a boost in self-esteem, expand your wardrobe when possible to include more of these kinds of clothes.

WRITE A LETTER TO YOUR YOUNGER SELF

Think about who you were when you were younger. It could be when you were in elementary school, middle school, or even just five years ago! You've learned so much about yourself and life since you were this age. If you were to travel through time and give yourself some advice or reassurance, what would you say? What fears did you have when you were younger that you have already faced and pulled through? What dreams or goals have you accomplished since then? Write a letter to your younger self now, letting them know what there is to love about where and who they will become.

_____

_____

_____

_____

_____

_____

_____

_____

_____

_____

_____

_____

DEVELOP DAILY GRATITUDE

Gratitude is an incredibly powerful tool. It can lift your spirits in low moments or even completely rewire your mindset. If you've been looking for one thing that's going to change your life, daily gratitude is your answer. Studies have shown that even simply acknowledging things you are grateful for each day can have a positive effect on your overall mental health over time.

Gratitude encourages you to focus on the positives in your life. The more you practice flexing your gratitude muscle, the more your brain will start to naturally look for the good instead of the bad in your daily life. This is especially powerful for self-love, helping you see the positive aspects in yourself rather than focusing on any negatives that may be affecting your confidence.

Try adding gratitude into your daily routine by spending simply 3–5 minutes thinking about what you are thankful for each day. If you can only think of one thing, that's okay! If you think of five or more, that's great too! What matters is you're carving out time in your day to focus on what you're grateful for, and you're training your brain to start focusing on the positives. This simple activity can help you see that even rough days may include some positive events!

MANAGE STRESS

One of the most important practices with self-love and overall self-care is managing your stress. Stress negatively affects not only your mental health but your physical health too! People who deal with continuous stress are more likely prone to headaches, high blood pressure, digestive issues, depression, and more. If you've noticed that stress has been negatively affecting your life and ability to extend love to yourself lately, it's time to start practicing some solid self-care activities.

There are many ways you can work on managing your stress. Meditation, for example, is an incredibly powerful tool for practicing mindfulness and calming anxiety—even if it's only for a few minutes. Journaling, exercise, or simply unplugging from social media for a certain amount of time on a regular basis can do wonders for your stress levels as well. Here are a few more options you can try:

Listen to calming music
Dance to your favorite song
Play with a pet
Take a nap
Focus on your breathing
Go for a walk
Practice yoga
Talk to a friend

Ultimately, you are going to need to figure out what methods work best for you.

CHECK IN WITH YOURSELF

When was the last time you tuned in to how you're feeling? It's so easy to get caught up in the hustle and bustle of day-to-day life that you forget to check in with how you actually feel. Are you feeling a little anxious because life is getting busy? Are you annoyed at anything? Is there anything in particular that's bringing you joy?

Taking some time to check in with yourself each day is important to help you stay in the moment and decide if what you're doing is right for you. When you start putting yourself first, you'll need to start by acknowledging how you're feeling and if any aspects of your life require adjustment or attention to help you feel better and live a healthier life. Checking in on a regular basis will help you feel better about yourself overall, and prioritizing yourself is the ultimate act of self-love.

Give it a try this week! Set an alarm for the same time each day. When it goes off, take a few moments to acknowledge how you feel. At the end of the week, notice if those check-ins helped you improve your mood or discover something new you didn't realize before!

RECITE AFFIRMATIONS

One powerful tool for building self-love is reciting affirmations. Positive affirmations are phrases that you repeat to yourself to challenge negative thoughts. The good news is, it's a very easy tool to use: Simply choose an area of your life to enhance with more positive thinking, and recite exactly what you want to believe.

For example, when working on your self-confidence, you could recite some of these affirmations each morning:

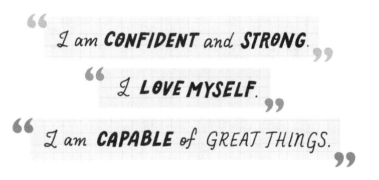

> *I am* **CONFIDENT** *and* **STRONG**.

> *I* **LOVE MYSELF**.

> *I am* **CAPABLE** *of* GREAT THINGS.

These affirmations help rewire your brain to start truly thinking and *feeling* what you're reciting to yourself each day. For the next three days, choose one affirmation and recite it to yourself three times when you wake up in the morning or when you go to bed (or both!). Each time you repeat your affirmations, try your best to truly feel and believe what you're saying. It may be tough at first, but over time you'll start to notice yourself shift to truly believing in your affirmations!

COMPLIMENT YOURSELF

What's the best compliment you've ever received from someone? Who was this person, and why did it mean so much to you?

_____

_____

_____

_____

Now think about this: How often do you give similar compliments to yourself? You may not say something formally, like "Self, you have a fantastic sense of humor," but how often are you genuinely gracious and complimentary in your self-talk? Not often? Maybe rarely, if ever? Let's kick off this habit! Write down three compliments to yourself right now:

_____

_____

_____

_____

_____

_____

_____

Keep this habit going beyond these pages. Try to compliment yourself at least once a day. Be your own biggest cheerleader!

TAKE FIVE DEEP BREATHS

Feeling absolutely anxious and overwhelmed? Are your thoughts racing a million miles an hour? Or no matter how hard you try, you can't seem to get a firm grasp of everything you need to do today? If you're consistently feeling stressed and overwhelmed, it's harder to focus on tuning in to what you need and want, which can impact your sense of self-love. In moments like these, one of the best things you can do is tune in to your breath.

Take a few moments right now to center yourself, and take five deep breaths.

In through your nose, and out through your mouth.

How do you feel after taking these deep breaths?

Next time you're feeling stressed or having trouble focusing, take a few moments to take these five deep breaths again. Simple deep-breathing exercises like these help decrease stress. When you take deep breaths, you're increasing the supply of oxygen to your brain, encouraging your mind to relax. Even a few short moments of breathing can make a powerful positive shift in your day!

GO ON A NATURE WALK

As our society has grown increasingly more dependent on technology, it's often easy to forget the power of nature. For example, in moments that you're feeling stressed, disconnected, or simply a bit off, unplugging and taking a nature walk can help you feel grounded again. Connecting with nature is one of the best forms of self-care, as you give yourself space to clear your head, breathe in the fresh air, and simply *be*. The more you give yourself the opportunity for these moments, the better you'll feel about yourself and the more love you'll be giving to someone who deserves it: you!

You don't need to go backpacking for a month and leave all of your worldly belongings behind; simply 10 minutes in the sunshine can greatly improve your mood. Even if your walk is a quick stroll through a park, letting your feet touch the grass, or digging your toes in the sand, reconnecting with nature can be a healing experience.

Plan one day this week where you'll explore and spend some time with nature. If you're near a body of water, you can visit a local pond or beach. Stuck in the city? Look for community gardens or nearby arboretums and nature centers where you can spend some time. Wherever you go, make sure you take time to intentionally connect with your surroundings. Be mindful of what you see, the sounds you hear, the scents you smell, and the critters you observe. Notice how you feel after your walk. If you notice a positive difference, continue exploring and start making nature walks a regular experience each week.

LISTEN TO YOUR SELF-TALK

Have you ever noticed how you talk to yourself? Not how you talk to yourself out loud, but how you speak to yourself in your head? What are the thought patterns that you notice you thinking about yourself throughout each day? Are you kind to yourself? Or harsh?

If you're unsure, think about how you approach a difficult project. Imagine this: You're struggling to manage all of the pieces, and nothing is coming easy. What are your opinions about yourself as you experience this? You may feel like it *shouldn't* be this hard. You may feel disappointed because you expected more from yourself, and start to think you're hopeless and unqualified.

Sound familiar? Now think of how you would talk to one of your loved ones if they were experiencing the same thing. Would you tell them they're hopeless and not worth the effort? Probably not! Your thoughts have an impact on how you feel about yourself. How you speak to yourself matters. We are usually our own harshest critics, but we don't have to continue this way! Next time you catch your brain spewing criticism, take a moment to give yourself some grace. You're trying your best, and you'll figure out whatever you need to do. You are more than capable. Treat yourself with love and respect.

LET GO OF INSECURITIES

Are there any parts about yourself that make you feel insecure?
Anything related to body image, your interests, or characteristics
that you aren't proud of showing the world?

_____

_____

_____

_____

_____

_____

In the next lines, write something positive about each of the
points you wrote just now. Whether it's something you truly believe
or not, find at least one way you can identify something good about
these insecurities.

_____

_____

_____

_____

_____

_____

The next time you find yourself feeling down and ashamed
about your insecurities, remind yourself of these positive state-
ments. Take a deep breath, and let go of the negative thoughts.
You're a beautiful, wonderful soul. See yourself in that light.

EXPRESS YOURSELF

Quick! Write down the first thing that comes to mind when asked these questions:

What is something you want to express about yourself but are too afraid to share?

_____

_____

_____

What's holding you back from talking about this? Are you afraid of someone else's opinion? Are you scared you'll fail?

_____

_____

_____

What is the worst thing that could happen if you did express yourself?

_____

_____

_____

What are the odds of this *truly* happening? They're probably slim. Take a chance and live your truth. The people who truly care about you will understand, and you deserve to live your best life without holding anything back.

LIST THE LOVE

What are all of the things that you love about yourself? If you find it hard to pinpoint anything, sit down and think about at least three things that you like about yourself. This can range from the color of your hair and movies you like to how you're good at a particular skill like playing an instrument or math—literally anything! Write it all down.

_____

_____

_____

_____

_____

_____

_____

_____

_____

_____

_____

_____

_____

Next time you're feeling down or insecure, refer back to this list and remind yourself why you're great. Add to the list every now and then, and grab another piece of paper if you run out of room.

DO IT ANYWAY

How many times have you let fear hold you back from trying some-thing new or taking a risk? When a loud inner critic tells you that you aren't capable of doing something or you're going to embarrass yourself, why wouldn't you listen to it? It's clearly got some truth to it, right?

Wrong. Your inner critic is often your ego trying to hold you back from getting hurt or failing. While it means well, it doesn't account for the big picture and all the positive possibilities that can come from taking chances outside of your comfort zone. It is purely operating out of survival instinct.

How do you take charge when your inner critic is taking over? Do the thing anyway.

Next time you're holding yourself back in any way because a lit-tle voice inside your head is trying to tell you that you're not capable or worthy enough, kindly tell it, "Thanks, but I've got this."

And do the thing anyway.

Any small steps toward facing this fear will help you build more confidence, leading you to feel more comfortable with trying new things over time. Imagine how much you could accomplish and grow if you didn't let that fear hold you back anymore!

STOP APOLOGIZING

Did you know that, on average, people apologize at least twenty times a day? That's over seven thousand times a year! Do you know how much *you* apologize? Apologies can sneak in without you even realizing you're saying them. For example, have you ever noticed yourself saying "sorry" before you simply ask someone a question at the store? Or when someone else bumps into you and it was clearly their fault?

Apologizing can become second nature after a while, but it's a dangerous habit that over time diminishes your self-confidence. On top of lowering your self-esteem, excessive apologizing dilutes the value of necessary apologies and leads to perceiving yourself as a burden all of the time. You do *not* need to apologize for taking up space or even minorly inconveniencing someone else. Life happens. You're human!

Instead of apologizing, switch to expressing gratitude.

FOR EXAMPLE, REPLACE

"I'm sorry for bothering you"

WITH

"Thank you for your help."

LOOK IN THE MIRROR

When you're struggling with loving yourself, it may be challenging to look in the mirror. If you're unhappy with who you are or how you look, learning to accept yourself and overcoming this kind of challenge is an important part of self-discovery.

Set a timer for 1 minute, and look at yourself in the mirror. What are the first thoughts that come to mind? Don't dwell on any of them, just write them down.

_____

_____

_____

_____

Now, if most of these initial thoughts were negative, set another timer for 1 minute, look in the mirror again, and notice three positive things you see. Write them down.

_____

_____

_____

_____

Continue this exercise for a few more days and notice how you feel. Although finding something positive may have been a challenge today, the more you practice, the easier it'll become, and the more you'll learn to accept the beautiful person you are, inside and out.

CELEBRATE YOURSELF

When was the last time you really celebrated the person you are? Everything that you've ever experienced, both the exciting moments and the tougher days, has helped you become the person that you are now. You are incredible. And on top of all of this, you're here now working on yourself so you can grow even more. Everything about yourself deserves celebration!

Write down ways you can celebrate yourself. Some examples include making time to do something fun that you love, writing a gratitude letter to yourself, or dancing to your favorite playlist. Schedule time to do one of these activities at least once a week. You deserve it!

_____

_____

_____

_____

_____

_____

_____

_____

_____

_____

_____

_____

_____

_____

REWRITE THE STORY

What is one recurrent insecurity that you think about often? What is one struggle that holds you back? For example, do you feel extremely self-conscious when you have to speak in front of an audience?

_____

_____

_____

Where did this insecurity come from? Was it from a past negative experience? Continuing the public speaking example, maybe you made several mistakes during a past presentation that made you feel embarrassed. Reflect on the origin of this insecurity.

_____

_____

_____

Rewrite this story. Knowing what you know, how can you rewrite this insecurity's origin story to be a learning experience? For example, making mistakes during speeches may have taught you how to better prepare for future presentations.

_____

_____

_____

Don't let your past define your present and future self in a way that holds you back!

TAP IN TO YOUR EMOTIONS

Take a moment and think about a version of yourself that's completely and fully self-confident. You accept every part of you and are content with where you are in life. What emotions would this fully confident version of yourself feel? Would you feel joyful? Adventurous? Excited? Proud? Write down all of the emotions in the following space.

_____

_____

_____

_____

Why not tap in to all of these emotions right now? What are some ways that you can start feeling these confident emotions today?

_____

_____

_____

_____

_____

_____

_____

_____

_____

FLIP THE SCRIPT

How many times have you held yourself back from trying something new or facing a challenge because you were scared of everything bad that could happen? For example, have you ever held back from speaking your mind in front of important people because you were scared you would be judged? Alternatively, maybe you've always wanted to try a new hobby, but you were worried you would fail.

Don't let these insecurities and worries hold you back from being the person you want to be. It's easy to let negative thoughts take over with the "what ifs" of a situation, but imagine the possibilities when you start framing those "what ifs" as positive scenarios. Instead of focusing on everything bad that could happen when trying something new or facing your fears, challenge yourself to think of at least three *good* things that could happen. Next time you're afraid to speak your mind, imagine how many people would benefit from your ideas, or the respect you might earn for sharing your unique opinion.

Challenge that inner critic and let it know that there are other possibilities—ones that could change your life for the better.

BECOME A STRONG TEAMMATE

Everyone has unique strengths, and this becomes even more apparent when you're with a group of people. Whether in a professional setting, an educational one, or simply with a group of peers, everyone can bring something unique to the group. Someone may be more creative and bring fresh ideas. Others may be adventurous and willing to take risks to try new things. Someone else may be a great critical thinker, able to analyze a problem everyone is dealing with in an objective way.

What do you bring to the team when you're in a group setting?

_____

_____

_____

_____

_____

_____

_____

_____

_____

_____

CREATE YOUR THEME SONG

In movies and TV shows, the background music matches how characters are feeling in various important scenes. When they're feeling sad, you'll hear slow, melancholy tunes in the background. When they're happy? Bright, upbeat, exciting melodies start playing as they go about their day.

What would your theme music be for the most confident version of yourself? Picture it: You're the main character, living as the fullest, most authentic version of you, fully accepting everything about who you are and where you are in life right now. What songs are playing in the background?

Create a playlist filled with music that fits the most confident version of yourself. This can be music you already know and love, popular songs you've heard in passing, or even new favorites. When you need an extra confidence boost, turn up this playlist as you tackle your day, or throw a solo dance party and lift your spirits even more!

RECRUIT YOUR INNER CIRCLE

Who are the people you trust the most and who know you better than anyone else? When you're working on building self-love during your self-discovery journey, outside recruits can be strong assets in your personal growth tool belt.

Think of a few people close to you who you trust. Ask them the first three positive characteristics or traits that come to mind when they think of you. For example, do they think you're authentic? Funny? Brave? Write down the answers here. Go over this list when you need extra confidence, knowing that this is how amazing you truly are to the most important people in your life.

_____

_____

_____

_____

_____

_____

_____

_____

_____

_____

_____

_____

_____

_____

EMBRACE THE UNEXPECTED

No matter how much you prepare, sometimes events don't turn out as you originally planned. While the unexpected can be terrifying, it isn't always bad. Dealing with the unexpected offers many learning moments that you may not realize you've already gone through!

Think back to a time when something that could have gone wrong, *did* go wrong.

How did you feel in that moment?

_____

_____

_____

_____

_____

What did you learn from that experience?

_____

_____

_____

_____

_____

You are far more capable than you realize. Don't let the unknown hold you back from taking on challenges and learning something new along the way.

PART 3

DISCOVER
YOUR
Purpose and
Passions

REMEMBER WHAT BRINGS YOU JOY

One of the first steps you can take to start discovering your purpose and passions is to reconnect with what lights you up inside. This can include forgotten hobbies, old interests, or school subjects you used to love. Take some extra time to really dig deep and uncover what you love to do without any expectations of turning it into a career. This is purely to acknowledge what can help enhance your life in a positive way.

Brain-dump everything that you love here. Don't hold back or judge; just write down everything that comes to mind.

_____

_____

_____

_____

_____

_____

_____

_____

_____

_____

Take a look at everything you wrote. Each item you identified indicates a potential passion or purpose that you can start exploring further. Keep in mind what lights you up inside—you never know where it will take you and what you'll learn along the way!

HELP SOMEONE ELSE

While you can have more than one purpose during your lifetime, one common factor is a part of every purpose: It's one way you can make a positive impact on the world around you. If you're struggling to discover a purpose that you can focus on right now, start with this end goal in mind. Take time to help someone else, whether it's by volunteering at a local animal shelter, offering to help a relative with a project around their house, tutoring your neighbor's child in a subject they're struggling with, or simply asking someone, "How can I help you?"

You never know what you'll learn about yourself when you take steps toward helping other people. You may find that you love to work with animals or that you enjoy working for a specific age group. Follow anything that particularly sparks your interest, and pursue it until you start to recognize that it's leading you to discovering your purpose. A bonus is that helping other people is a fulfilling way to spend your time!

REVISIT YOUR SCHOOL DAYS

Reflecting back on your classes in school is an excellent way to reconnect with something that you may have been passionate about when you were younger. Think back to elementary school or later, in high school or college. Was there a particular subject that you were excited to learn about each day? Did you work on a project that piqued your interest or that you enjoyed doing more than all of the other homework assignments you dealt with? There's a reason you were interested in these things when you were younger. It's easy to get distracted by other goals and aspirations as you get older, but at the core, you may still be excited about the subjects that interested you in school.

Once a subject comes to mind, start exploring it this week. Take time to look up books, podcasts, or *YouTube* videos to explore the subject more.

STOP THE CLOCK

Are you ever so focused on something that you don't even realize that time is flying by? Do you ever get so lost in projects or hobbies that you even forget to eat? While it's never recommended to skip important meals, stay aware this week and notice if you work on anything that has you feeling this way—like time is fleeting simply because you're enjoying what you're doing.

These moments when you feel like time is standing still can be clear signs that you're working on something you're passionate about, and it could lead you to finding your purpose. These activities are special, because far too often we spend time on projects we don't enjoy or even dread. When you find tasks that make you lose track of time, make note of how you can invest more of your everyday routine into them. Life is too short not to spend time on what you're truly passionate about!

LEAVE YOUR LEGACY

How do you want other people to remember you when you're gone? Do you want them to look back fondly on how you were an ambitious go-getter who accomplished all of your dreams? Or maybe you'd love to be remembered for your caring heart, how you were always there for people when they needed you. Neither of these legacies is "incorrect." What matters is what feels the most aligned for you.

What legacy do you want to leave in your life?

_____

_____

_____

_____

_____

_____

_____

_____

Are you currently living your life aligned with this desired legacy? If not, this is your sign to make a change and start taking steps toward building your dream future. This legacy you just wrote down can help you uncover your ultimate purpose in your life. Keep this in mind as you continue to explore, and see what avenues come up that help align you further with your desired legacy.

FEEL THE PULL

As you go through your everyday routine, even when life feels monotonous, what are some things that you find yourself naturally drawn toward? Think of the natural instincts that you regularly follow, such as researching topics you find fascinating for fun or frequently checking in on certain types of current events. You can take the question a step further as well: Are there any hobbies you loved when you were younger that you disconnected from at some point? Reconnecting might bring you joy again! Any of these interests can unlock potential passions that you have yet to explore further.

Throughout the week, notice if you find anything you commonly choose to do because you simply enjoy doing it. For example, whenever you feel stuck in the boring day-to-day, what is one thing you wish you were doing? Once you capture that pull, dig a little deeper. You never know what passions and/or purpose you might discover!

OWN WHAT MAKES YOU UNIQUE

Sometimes your purpose or passions are hidden within you, waiting to be recognized. How do you recognize them? Think about your unique talents. What are some things that you are naturally good at that are a bit different from what you see in other people? For example, maybe you've always been naturally gifted at listening when other people need someone to talk to, or you excel at sharing important stories that need to be told through writing. Whatever your unique talents, identify one (or more!) and keep it in mind when you're exploring your passions. You never know where it might lead you to in the future!

What are some of your unique talents?

_____

_____

_____

_____

_____

_____

_____

_____

_____

_____

_____

CREATE A BUCKET LIST

Have you ever created a bucket list? A bucket list is a list of things you want to do or accomplish throughout your life. They often include vacation destinations, big dreams, and major milestones, such as having a family. In addition to using a bucket list to live an exciting and fulfilled life, what you include and explore can open doors to helping you uncover what you're passionate about in your life.

What's on your bucket list? Write down everything you want to do in your life in the lines that follow. After you've written this list down, think about how you're currently living your life. Are you following any paths that align with this bucket list? If not, how can you start prioritizing these items so you start living a life that's more aligned with what you want?

_____

_____

_____

_____

_____

_____

_____

_____

_____

_____

_____

PAINT A PERFECT SATURDAY

It's the most wonderful day of the week: Saturday! (Or if you have a day off on a different day of the week, that day!) What would your absolute perfect Saturday look like? If you had all of the money and time in the world, how would you spend your day off? Describe what this day would look like here:

_____

_____

_____

_____

_____

Do your Saturdays usually look like this? If not, what are some steps you can take to start aligning your days off to match this perfect day as well as any restrictions allow?

_____

_____

_____

_____

_____

_____

The more you align your life with the ideal day you wrote down, the more aligned you'll become with your purpose and passions in life.

GET A SECOND OPINION

When you're working on discovering what you're passionate about or finding your purpose(s), getting a second opinion from an outside source is a great way to receive different perspectives. A friend or family member may see some potential in you or notice something that you  excel at that you've never considered before. For example, maybe you've never noticed that you're great at giving advice to other people or that you're a good listener. These traits that weren't originally at the forefront of your mind could play into discovering a purpose or passion in your life.

Reach out to three people you are close to, such as friends, relatives, coworkers, classmates, mentors, coaches—anyone! Ask them what they believe are some of your best traits or talents. What do they think you're good at? What do they admire about you?

Keep in mind, you aren't required to take everything they say to heart. If someone tells you that you're talented in ways that don't excite you, those don't have to be your passions! Any opinions that feel aligned with your instincts (even unexpected ones!) can help guide you toward learning about yourself and what you want in life.

REMOVE FAILURE FROM THE EQUATION

What would you do if you knew you couldn't fail? It's easy to let your fear of failure hold you back from pursuing something. If one reason that you stay in your comfort zone is that you're afraid if you venture out of it, you'll fail, congrats! You're human! However, you can't let this fear continue to hold you back from pursuing things that may turn into passions or even a deeper purpose.

Imagine how your life would be if failure weren't an option. What would you do?

_____

_____

_____

_____

What are some first steps you can take to making this life you just painted into a reality?

_____

_____

_____

_____

All of this is possible. Don't let your fear hold you back!

TRY SOMETHING NEW

If you're struggling to discover your passions or find your purpose, it's time to explore new options. When was the last time you tried something completely different? There are so many ways you can participate in new things. Look up new options for different hobbies online, sign up for a class to learn a new skill, watch a documentary in a genre you usually don't watch, or visit a restaurant that serves food that you're not used to eating on a regular basis. The opportunities are endless!

Each time you try something new, be present and truly experience what you're pursuing. You may discover something you truly love that you wouldn't have noticed before! Take it a step further and write down notes about your experience, identifying what you liked and disliked, or what you'd like to explore even more. Taking one step in a new direction can lead you down a path of incredible self-discovery.

CREATE A VENN DIAGRAM

When you're trying to discover your purpose, you may find it's hard to keep track of what *you* actually want versus what others want for you. If you're feeling this way, it's time to put your thoughts on paper.

Create a Venn diagram with three circles that all overlap in the middle, and label them "Passions," "Talents," and "What's Needed." When it comes to finding your purpose, you're likely to find something that feels aligned with you when you combine what you love to do with what you're good at and what the world needs right now so you can make a positive impact on those around you. Where do your passions, your talents, and what's needed overlap?

LISTEN TO A PODCAST

Podcasts have skyrocketed in popularity over recent years. And it's no wonder—there are podcasts for nearly every topic you can imagine! As you adventure through your self-discovery journey, exploring new podcasts is a great way to start learning about different subjects; potential hobbies, skills, or careers; news; and so much more. And you can easily listen to podcast episodes while you're already doing something else! For example, listening while working out, cleaning your house, and driving are popular ways to learn something new from podcasts without carving out extra time in your day.

Find a podcast platform that you'd like to use to explore new shows and episodes. Some of the popular ones are Apple Podcasts (for iPhone users), Spotify, Pandora, Amazon Music Podcasts, and Google Podcasts, but there are countless options out there. Search a subject that you're interested in and select a few shows to try out this week. If you find a show you particularly enjoy, explore its episodes further. Don't be afraid to listen to something completely new every once in a while too!

THINK BEYOND THE PAYCHECK

One misconception people often have about finding your purpose is that it should correlate directly with your career. Do you have similar expectations? Are you searching for the "perfect" job that's going to fully embody your biggest passions and propel your ultimate purpose?

First of all, that's a lot of pressure to put on yourself and your career! While some people may be able to find this "perfect" occupation, the reality is that work is...work! Your purpose might be something completely different, and that is absolutely okay. It is completely fine if your job is simply something you do to earn a living. In fact, your job may give you the financial freedom to pursue your purpose and passions without the pressure of monetizing them!

If you've been stuck correlating your career with your passions or purpose, change this connection today. What are some things that can be your purpose but aren't necessarily associated with a job? Explore these options, and see what possibilities have been hiding behind the occupational wall you previously built up. You never know what you'll discover.

TAKE A CLASS

When was the last time you took a class outside of school? Have you ever signed up to learn something new beyond your regular curriculum, whether you're currently attending school or already graduated? There are so many types of classes you can take to explore something new or further hone skills you enjoy. Whether you're a creative who loves to write, paint, or play music, or you're more on the analytical side and love to research and dive into data, you can find plenty of opportunities for both online and in-person classes to explore new passions!

Go online and research a few different courses you can take either online or in person in a subject you're interested in exploring. Local community centers in your area may offer in-person events. And websites such as *MasterClass* and *Udemy* have a variety of options to learn more about different topics and skills. Sign up for at least one class this week, and stay present when you attend. Notice if there's anything in particular you love, and don't be afraid to continue taking new classes to learn even more about yourself and explore new skills!

SMILE

When it comes to connecting with what you're passionate about, even the simplest things like knowing what makes your smile light up can lead you toward discovering your passions and even the road toward your purpose. Don't discount those moments or activities that make you smile—even if they aren't necessarily your biggest passions. Whether it's your pet, a loved one, your favorite song, a funny quote—anything that brings a smile to your face matters. Remembering what makes you happy can brighten both your day and someone else's.

What are at least five things that make you smile?

ELIMINATE THE "SHOULDS"

When it comes to learning exactly what you want and following your unique purpose and passions, there's one word that you need to eliminate from your vocabulary immediately: *should*.

The word *should* holds you back from doing what you actually want to do with your life. How many times have you pursued something because you thought it was what you "should" do? If you continued to pursue higher education, was it in an area that you really wanted to study or one that you thought you "should" study? Have you ever avoided going after a goal because someone said you "shouldn't" do it? These perceived obligations and no-nos often originate in family or societal expectations.

Stop listening to these "shoulds" in your life. Tune in to what you actually *want*. Pay attention to your thoughts this week. When you make decisions, check to see if any lingering "shoulds" are influencing you. If you notice any, reflect on where they came from, and then tune in with your intuition and recognize if it's what you truly want for yourself. Following this true instinct beyond the "should" will help you live a much more fulfilled life than any "should" ever could give you!

TAKE IT EASY

What are some things that you find come easily for you? Has anyone ever said "You're a natural!" at something?

Maybe writing has always been something that comes easily for you. Sure, there are days where you're creatively frustrated, don't use the best grammar, or simply don't feel like doing it—but it's still something that overall comes naturally to you. Think of something that you've enjoyed doing for most of your life—even if, when you're doing it on a professional level, it may not be fun—and that coincidentally isn't super challenging for you.

So what are some things that come easily to you? Think about your daily tasks at work, classes you've had in school, projects or hobbies you've participated in, anything! Whatever comes to mind, those skills are likely signs pointing you toward discovering a purpose and/or passion in life.

PONDER YOUR "WHY"

As you go through your self-discovery journey, identifying your "why" is a key step toward staying true to yourself. *Why* do you want to find your purpose? *Why* are you searching for your passions? *Why* is this whole process so important to you? Once you start connecting with your purpose and passions, you can integrate your answers to these questions into your overall "why" for your personal development journey, propelling you forward when you're pursuing your biggest goals.

Maybe you're searching for purpose because you no longer feel like you have a direction, or you're stuck in a rut and feel totally lost and discouraged about life. Or maybe you're tired of everyone else's opinions and want to learn what makes *you* happy.

What's your "why"?

_____

_____

_____

_____

_____

_____

_____

_____

_____

ANSWER LOOMING QUESTIONS

What questions do you find yourself thinking about on a regular basis? For example, what are you constantly curious about or wanting to research? Maybe you wonder why certain people are treated unfairly in your society, or you ponder the best ways to be a loving and supportive partner. Or perhaps you want to know the best places to explore in this world to learn new things. These questions that remain in your head can reveal what's most important to you—what you value—as well as your purpose or things you're passionate about.

What unanswered questions do you think about often?

_____

_____

_____

_____

_____

_____

_____

_____

_____

_____

_____

_____

SERVE WITH YOUR TALENTS

When it comes to connecting with your overall purpose in life (you can have more than one as well!), the ultimate goal is to discover what it is that you love to do that also has a positive impact on other people. An excellent way to do this is by using your naturally gifted talents. Earlier in this journal, you explored a few exercises targeted toward pinpointing your talents and what makes you unique. How can you use those talents and unique qualities to serve and help other people?

Maybe you're naturally good at interacting with animals; you can use those talents to volunteer at an animal shelter or take care of foster pets while they're waiting for their forever home. Or you're naturally good at teaching other people; you can volunteer to tutor at a youth center or school. The opportunities are endless!

Once you've pinpointed at least one talent and a way to use it to help others, take action. Learn the steps you need to take to officially become a volunteer. Choose a location to serve. Don't just sit on your talents and your new awareness of how you can help—go make a difference!

FIND THE COMMONALITIES

Have you ever noticed anything in common among your various interests? For example, a trend of specific topics when choosing what books to read and TV shows to watch? Perhaps you love a specific genre of music or catch yourself drawn to similar types of poetry. Discovering these commonalities can be a key to pinpointing larger passions.

What things do you really enjoy? These can be specific books, music, movie genres, poems, activities, hobbies—literally anything. Write them all down, and be specific (e.g., social justice documentaries and autobiography books). When you're finished, circle all of the interests that have something in common. Do you notice any new trends? Explore these themes further on your own.

WILLINGLY SUFFER

Everything that you do in life takes some measure of sacrifice. When you choose to spend your time on one thing, you're actively choosing to not focus on something else. This isn't necessarily bad, it's simply the truth. On top of this, every goal or project that you work toward completing is going to come with its own hardships. Whether you're striving to run an 8-minute mile and pushing through that last lap to shave off precious seconds, or learning a new song on the piano and getting tired of trying to master a complicated chord, you'll deal with some level of suffering at some point in your journey.

The big question is, What are *you* willing to suffer through?

What struggles are you willing to deal with in order to achieve your dreams? Identifying them will unveil what's most important to you, and this can lead you to understand what you're passionate about in life. Keep an eye out for what you're willing to endure. The more you understand why you're suffering through something, the more you'll see that it comes from a place of passion and love, which helps you ultimately have a more fulfilling life!

CONNECT WITH YOUR INTUITION

A common trend you'll notice within this self-discovery journal is the importance of trusting your own intuition when you make decisions. However, this can be a terrifying task if you're not used to listening to your own instincts and trusting yourself. After all, who are you going to blame if you make a mistake or fail? Listening to other people and doing what they say is always so much easier.

Or is it? Think about it. When was the last time you listened to your intuition? What happened when you did? How did you feel?

_____

_____

_____

_____

_____

_____

_____

_____

_____

_____

_____

Trusting your own instincts can be scary, but it helps you better align your life with your purpose and passions, helping you live an authentic life!

REWORK YOUR TALENTS

Now that you've taken time to explore your natural gifts and what you enjoy, use what you've discovered to explore new approaches to life and even newfound passions. What does this mean? Use the skills that you apply to things you already enjoy, and try to apply them to other parts of your life. For example, if you love to play sports, you could take those natural gifts and passions and start hiking outdoors or going trail running.

What is one passion and/or talent of yours that you can repurpose to explore something new?

_____

_____

_____

_____

_____

_____

_____

_____

_____

_____

_____

_____

Now go try it yourself this week!

RELEASE UNANSWERED QUESTIONS

Do you ever find yourself reflecting on any big existential questions about life? Looming, unanswered questions that don't have any easy answer? Some examples can include, "What is the meaning of life?" or "What's the real reason why I'm here?"

Write down any of these questions that you've thought about.

_____

_____

_____

_____

_____

_____

_____

_____

The truth is, there's no single answer to these questions. There's even a chance that you'll never find any concrete answer. But that's okay! You don't _have_ to know the answers in order to live a meaningful life. What truly matters at the end of the day is that you're following your heart and staying connected with what's important to _you_ each day.

Next time you find yourself hung up on an existential question, allow yourself to reflect a little, but ultimately accept that you may never know the answer.

DON'T SHUT UP

Is there anything that you absolutely cannot stop talking about? Something that you get really excited to share with others or even teach people all about at every opportunity? It lights you up, and you may even be concerned that other people are annoyed that you won't shut up about it! For example, if you *love* to travel to new places, you may find yourself constantly giving other people advice about finding the best flights or telling stories about your latest adventures.

What do you *love* to talk about? Why do you love to talk about it?

_____

_____

_____

_____

_____

_____

_____

_____

Congratulations: You just identified one of your passions!

MAKE MISTAKES

You do *not* need to be an expert when it comes to pursuing your passions and living with purpose. In fact, part of the beauty of living life aligned with your passions and purpose is the experience of pursuing them in general. Enjoying the journey, rather than the desired destination, is just as sweet as fulfilling your goals. During this process, you are going to make mistakes. And that's okay! In fact, it's better that you do make mistakes, because they're excellent ways to learn. If you're following your passion of teaching children, traveling, or writing, for example, the process of participating in all of those passions is where the beauty of living with purpose shines.

Take chances this week when working on your passions, and don't be afraid to make mistakes. You do not need to be an expert at what you're pursuing. What matters is that you feel aligned with purpose and passionate about what you do, and you're enjoying life in the process.

FIND YOUR PEOPLE

One of the most beneficial parts of pursuing your passions and living with purpose is finding like-minded people who can be a part of your journey. This doesn't necessarily mean they have the same exact passions and/or purpose as you, but they understand how important living life in the way *you* want is for you. These are the people you can go to when celebrating the big wins, but also when you need someone to lean on when the journey gets bumpy. They want the best for you and aren't afraid to give you some tough love when you need it. But this isn't just a one-way relationship—you would support them in turn on their own self-discovery journey.

Have some people in mind? Take some time this week to reach out to them and ask about how their journey is going. The more support you give to the right people who truly care, the more you'll receive in return.

DON'T MAKE IT DIFFICULT

People have a tendency to make things more complicated than they need to be. But that's the beauty of discovering your passions and purpose—it doesn't have to be hard. Sure, there's a learning curve, and you're going to make mistakes, but it doesn't have to feel like an uphill battle. There's a difference between finding your footing with learning something new and finding everything that can possibly go wrong, and believing that it will.

Constantly focusing on the negatives when pursuing your passions and purpose is only going to make things harder in the long run. If you've found yourself falling into this trap, take time this week to focus on how you can let it be easy. You're allowed to let things flow in the direction they need to go. You're allowed to let things be easy for once in your life. What's meant to be will happen. Trust the process and enjoy it!

PART 4

DISCOVER
YOUR
Motivations

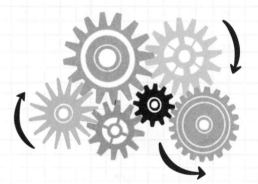

FIND YOUR RHYTHM

Did you know that everyone has more energy to be productive at different times of the day? For example, when you wake up early in the morning, are you energized and ready to tackle the day? Or are you barely slugging along until you've had your daily cup of coffee? Alternatively, are you able to stay up late at night or can you barely keep your eyes open past 10 p.m.?

If you already know that you're an early bird or night owl, use this to your advantage! Schedule your day (if possible) according to your natural energy levels. If you're more of a morning person, plan to tackle the projects that require the most focus and effort early in the day. Take a little longer to wake up? Work on the things that require the least brainpower first, then address the more intensive projects in the afternoon. Your overall productivity will get a boost when you work *with* your body's natural energy flow instead of forcing yourself to trudge through when you're slowing down. Try it out this week and see if you notice a difference!

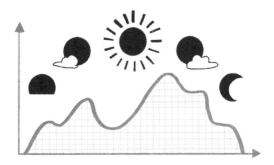

BLOCK IT OUT

On days when you feel completely overwhelmed, can't focus on one task at a time, or don't even know where to start because you have so much on your plate, it's time to implement time blocking.

Time blocking is a method by which you schedule out your time in "blocks" and solely focus on what you specifically scheduled during that time frame. No multitasking, no getting distracted with emails, and no changing course to do something else at the same time. Multitasking isn't effective (it's not even truly possible to focus completely on more than one thing at a time), so focusing on one project or task for a specific period can help improve your productivity and help you feel less overwhelmed at the same time. In addition, you'll know exactly what you have on your plate at any given moment, and you won't need to make decisions or find motivation multiple times throughout your day. Simply plan out your main priorities that you need to work on, and don't get pulled in a different direction unless it's an emergency.

Not only will this help your productivity, but you'll have a clear definition of how much time you have in your day for other activities or if you can take on more tasks or events. If not, you can easily show someone your schedule to create healthy boundaries about your time.

CREATE A MORNING ROUTINE

Do you have a morning routine? Morning routines can be extremely beneficial toward setting up your day for success. Even if you aren't the brightest ray of sunshine in the morning, a routine can help you reset your mind and align your mood in a positive, motivated way. If you've heard about morning routines before, you may have heard of elaborate ones that last over an hour. Don't get intimidated! A routine can be as simple as having a quiet moment with a cup of coffee or spending 10 minutes journaling your thoughts.

Think about some simple activities that bring you joy, and start adding at least one of these activities at a time into your morning routine. After a week of trying something new, reflect on how you feel. How is your energy? Have you experienced any mindset shifts? Have you been more productive than you had been previously? Adjust as needed until you have an ideal process that starts your day on a positive note that feels right for you.

MAKE A MOTIVATIONAL PLAYLIST

Music is powerful. One song can completely alter your mood in a matter of minutes. Whether you're watching a movie and the sad soundtrack moves you to tears, or a song from your childhood causes you to jump up and sing like a fool, music triggers incredible emotions. So why not use music as a tool to help you be more productive?

Athletes and performing artists often listen to a set of songs specifically to help them get motivated before a big game or performance. Try this yourself! Create a playlist of songs that get you excited to tackle whatever you have in front of you. Pick some tunes that you already know help boost your mood, but explore related artists and albums that you may not have discovered yet as well. Once you have the full playlist under your belt, anytime you need an extra push of motivation, listen to these songs and get ready to tackle your day!

MEDITATE FOR PRODUCTIVITY

Have you heard of *monkey mind*? It's a term used to describe a restless mind in which thoughts bounce around like a monkey and can't settle down. If you ever have those days when you need to get a lot done and, despite knowing how to prioritize your time, you simply can't get your mind to focus, you may be suffering from monkey mind. Whether it's because you're feeling anxious, overwhelmed, or even just really excited to tackle everything on your to-do list, monkey mind is going to hold you back from truly being productive.

Enter meditation.

Meditation is an excellent practice to help you calm your mind and refocus so you can be more productive. You can find guided meditations online or in popular meditation apps such as Insight Timer and Calm that are specifically created to help boost productivity. The next time you're struggling to focus, search for "meditation for productivity" online or in an app and try one out for yourself. If one meditation doesn't work well for you, don't give up! You'll find many different styles and lengths of meditations as well. And calming your mind is simply tougher some days than others. Meditation is proven to help improve your focus and overall mindset. Even 5 minutes of meditation could help boost your motivation and be more productive!

IDENTIFY YOUR VERSION OF SUCCESS

What does success look like to you? Even if you share the same ultimate goals as others, you'll likely define success differently. Some value excelling in their career, some view a successful life as having a family, and some define success as traveling to as many destinations as possible. All of these versions of success are valid. What's yours? Think about your values, your dreams, and anything else that's important to you. When do you feel the most successful?

TURN ON THE TOMATO TIMER

Did you know that the average human mind can truly focus for only about 25 minutes at a time? Our attention spans are getting shorter and shorter all the time, which makes things difficult if you need to focus for a long period of time on a project or long-term task. The good news? There's a time management technique that you can use to help you focus that takes advantage of your short-term attention span: the Pomodoro Technique.

Productivity expert Francesco Cirillo developed the Pomodoro Technique when he realized he could use his tomato-shaped kitchen timer (*pomodoro* is Italian for "tomato") to break up tasks into manageable, focused time periods. When you use the Pomodoro Technique, you'll work in 25-minute bursts of laser focus, with 5-minute breaks in between these "sprints." After four sessions of 25-minute sprints, you'll take a 20- to 30-minute break.

Here's the full breakdown:

1. *25 minutes working*
2. *5 minutes break*
3. *25 minutes working*
4. *5 minutes break*
5. *25 minutes working*
6. *5 minutes break*
7. *25 minutes working*
8. *20-30 minutes break*

Still have work to do after this set? Start over and continue with the cycle until you're done!

ESTABLISH AN EVENING ROUTINE

People often talk about how important a morning routine is, but establishing an evening routine can be just as beneficial—especially for the days when you've had a lot on your plate, are overwhelmed, or are simply feeling a little off. Having a routine in place as you wind down for the night can help you feel more grounded and relaxed before you go to sleep. Your evening routine doesn't have to be anything extravagant; just establish some simple habits that train your mind to realize that when you go through this specific routine, it's time to slow down and get ready to end your day.

You may already have some evening habits in place, such as washing your face and brushing your teeth. If you know you need some more steps added to the routine to help you relax more before you sleep, try adding one more step to your current routine each week. For example, add the habit of turning off your phone (or putting it in airplane mode) before you start your nightly habits. This way, you don't have any distractions or additional exposure to blue light that may keep you awake longer. Next, add 5–10 minutes of meditation, or filling up a glass of water to keep by your bed to drink when you wake up. Little efforts like this can help you set yourself up for more success tomorrow.

BRAIN-DUMP AND PRIORITIZE

When you have tons of responsibilities to balance, it can be hard to prioritize what's swirling around in your head. Everything seems like a priority, but the reality is that some tasks are more important than others.

Here are steps to take when you're struggling to prioritize:

 1 Write down everything you need to do. Brain-dump them all here:

_____

_____

_____

_____

_____

_____

 2 Take a look at your brain dump and write down each task's deadline. Circle the ones that are the soonest and most urgent.

Congrats: You now have your priorities! Focus on these tasks first, and organize your days based on these most important projects. Don't worry about the others until you're done and ready to tackle something else on the list.

FIND YOUR OWN MOTIVATION

You're not always going to feel motivated. In fact, you cannot rely on general motivation in order to be productive. Sometimes you need to find your own motivation in order to take on your tasks for the day. How? Break down everything you need to do into individual steps:

_____

_____

_____

_____

_____

_____

_____

_____

_____

_____

_____

_____

Now do the first step—just start. Set a timer and make sure you commit to it for at least 10 minutes!

REMOVE DAILY DISTRACTIONS

Did you know that the average person checks their phone fifty-eight times per day? That's a lot of distractions that you may not even realize you're dealing with on a daily basis! If you notice that you're struggling to stay focused and productive when needed, it's time to take a close look at what's pulling your attention away from your responsibilities. Removing even the simplest distractions can make a huge difference for helping improve your overall focus.

For example, removing the notifications from social media apps on your phone will decrease the likelihood of grabbing your phone if someone messages you, "likes" a photo, comments on a status update, and so on. You'll see these notifications when you go out of your way to open the app, instead of letting the app pull you in. Another distraction could be noises from your external environment. If you get distracted by conversations of people around you, use headphones and play some focus music.

Pay close attention to what distracts you during your day, and take simple steps to block out that distraction to help improve your overall productivity.

SIMPLIFY YOUR LIFE

Your self-discovery journey and the new habits you build along the way can be an exciting experience! But it's easy to feel extremely motivated in the beginning, wanting to accomplish all the things that you're inspired to tackle, and then slowly grow burned out and discouraged because you're expecting so much from yourself right away. Real change takes time!

If you find yourself in this motivated-to-burnout cycle, it's time to simplify your next steps. Pick one main goal that you would like to focus on, and break it down into all of the action steps and smaller habits you would need to change in order to achieve this goal. For example, if you want to train to run a marathon, start with walking a half mile each day. Then increase it to 1 mile each day, or speed up your pace to complete the half mile in less time. The key is to get into the basic habit first, then move on to challenging yourself to build upon each of these small habits. Before you know it, you're in the race!

SET YOURSELF UP FOR SUCCESS

How often do you prepare for the next day or the upcoming week ahead of time? For example, do you ever lay out your clothes the night before or meal-prep your week's lunches on Sundays? If you haven't done this before, prepping ahead of time can be a great way to save yourself time and set yourself up for success.

Imagine how much time you'll save if you choose what to wear the night before, organize your space right before you go to sleep, or premake easy meals for your workweek. You'll no longer have to spend time making decisions about what you need to wear first thing in the morning, cooking your meals during the weekdays, and straightening up your living room. How freeing does that sound?

Today, choose one thing you can do to set yourself up for success tomorrow. Slowly build on this new habit and see how much you can do to save your future self some time.

DANCE IT OUT

Have some important tasks you need to take care of but feel absolutely unmotivated and stuck? Everything in your body is screaming that you don't want to do what you need to do, but you don't really have a choice—it needs to be done now. What can you do to get out of this funk?

Throw a solo dance party!

Find your absolute favorite upbeat songs, and dance like there's no tomorrow. Don't worry about looking weird; simply get lost in the music and let the beat take you to a new level of energy. Music is powerful, and getting your blood flowing through movement is an excellent way to clear your mind and refocus on what you need to do. Even if you're not having a low day right now, make a playlist for those days that you do need the extra energy boost. Your future self will thank you!

ALIGN WITH YOUR FUTURE

Take a moment to think about your standard day and your daily habits. Now think about your long-term goals—do your daily habits align with these goals? Even some of the smallest routines can add up and help you accomplish bigger goals. If they don't align, what are some new habits you can start forming to help you work toward your ideal future?

_____

_____

_____

_____

_____

_____

_____

_____

_____

_____

Choose one of these new habits and start building it into your daily routine one day at a time. Be patient with yourself if you don't adhere to it every day—habits take time! Each day you work on it counts, even if you miss a day or two.

SCHEDULE FUN

When you write down your to-do list or create a schedule for your day, how often do you include something fun? It's easy to get caught up in the mandatory priorities of each day, but don't forget to make time for things you enjoy. Making fun activities a priority in your regular schedule not only brings more joy into your life but also helps you feel more motivated overall, giving your schedule more balance and giving you something to look forward to each day!

Write down a list of activities you enjoy doing, and include at least one of these activities in your schedule each day to make sure you're still having some fun!

BE AWARE OF BURNOUT

Once you have your motivation in place and you're being incredibly productive, it's important to remember to pace yourself. Whether it's scheduling regular breaks, taking mental health days, or prioritizing self-care activities, rest and rejuvenation absolutely need to be a part of your regular routine even when you're highly motivated and working hard.

Otherwise, you risk oncoming burnout. Burnout means you've been overworking yourself and dealing with stress to the point of exhaustion, but it's more than just feeling very tired. If you feel at risk of burnout, keep an eye out for some of these signs:

EMOTIONAL EXHAUSTION:

You're feeling drained and tired, and don't have the energy to do your regular work throughout the day.

PHYSICAL PAIN:

You're experiencing headaches or stomach problems from stress.

DECLINE IN PERFORMANCE:

You're starting to fall behind in the quality of your work, finding it difficult to concentrate for a long period of time.

If you're experiencing any of these signs, it's time to truly prioritize your self-care. In the long run, this will help you be more consistent with your productivity and improve your overall performance.

WRITE YOUR OWN DEFINITION

If you asked a group of people how they would define the word *productivity* in relation to their own life, you'd likely hear multiple interpretations of the term. To one person, being productive means doing something directly correlated with achieving a goal or fulfilling a responsibility as much as possible. A different person might see productivity as doing what you truly *need* to do at a given time, whether those needs last as little as a few hours or the entire day.

What does productivity mean to you? Write your own definition here:

productivity *noun*

FIND BALANCE

Sometimes the concept of work-life balance seems like an unattainable fantasy. How are you supposed to work full-time and balance your social life, health, and other routine responsibilities equally? Is that even possible?

The answer: It depends. What does work-life balance mean to you? Maybe it includes spending time on self-care and participating in your favorite hobby every day after work, or maybe it's simply making sure that you do one thing for yourself each day that makes you happy, even for just 5 minutes.

What would a balanced day look like for you?

_____

_____

_____

_____

_____

_____

_____

_____

_____

_____

_____

_____

AUTOMATE

How many decisions do you think you make each day? Inc.com reports that the average adult makes around 32,000 decisions per day. That's a *lot*! On top of this, think about how much energy it takes to make decisions. When you're exhausted from a stressful day, the last thing you want to do is choose what to make for dinner. One great hack for productivity and motivation is to automate and simplify the small choices you make each day.

Think about all of the decisions you make on a regular basis: What time you wake up in the morning, if you're going to work out, what you're going to eat, your outfits, what errands you need to run, rooms to clean...the list goes on! Now imagine how freeing it would feel if you were to free up those daily decisions. Here are a few ways you can try doing this right now:

- ✔ Choose your outfits ahead of time for the next day (or the entire week!)
- ✔ Set a recurring alarm and stick to it each morning
- ✔ Prep enough food to have leftovers for meals throughout the week
- ✔ Set up automatic bill payments
- ✔ Plan out your workouts for the week ahead of time

Try a couple of these options this week and see how you feel!

QUIT PROCRASTINATING

Everyone knows that procrastinating is a bad habit to have and a hard one to break. It's easy to identify that you're a chronic procrastinator and *should* break the habit...but *how*? If you're always the person waiting until the last day to write a paper due at midnight or finishing a project for work minutes before the deadline, it's time to get down to the root cause of *why* you're always procrastinating.

Take some time to truly reflect on why you procrastinate. Are you a perfectionist who's scared to take action and do something wrong? Do you need to work on your organizational skills? Be honest with yourself. Once you identify the "why," you can start taking steps toward finally breaking this habit once and for all.

_____

_____

_____

_____

_____

_____

_____

_____

_____

_____

_____

PRIORITIZE YOUR GOALS

Before you start diving into all of the goals that you have in mind for your future, you need to take a quick step back and prioritize what you need to focus on first. Trying to go after multiple goals at once can easily lead to overwhelm and burnout, which is counterproductive to all of the work you've been doing throughout your self-discovery journey.

List all of the goals you want to accomplish.

_____

_____

_____

_____

Out of this list, which are your top three most important goals? Why these three?

_____

_____

_____

Brainstorm how you're going to pursue these goals. Then take this brainstorm and organize it into your schedule to ensure you're focused on your main objectives!

_____

_____

_____

SET SMART GOALS

The best approach to goal-setting is creating **SMART** goals, which means your goals are specific, measurable, attainable, relevant, and time-based. Let these prompts guide you as you set your first **SMART** goal!

What is your **SPECIFIC** overall goal? (Example: I am going to run a mile in 8 minutes.)

_____

What is the **MEASURABLE** sign that you've achieved your goal? (Example: 8-minute mile)

_____

Is your goal realistically **ATTAINABLE**? (Not too low that you're not pushing yourself but not too high that it's nearly impossible.)
YES / NO

_____

How is your goal **RELEVANT** for your overall vision for your future? (Example: Running fits into my vision for a healthy lifestyle.)

_____

What **TIME** frame are you planning to achieve this goal? (Example: three months)

_____

Congratulations, you just created your first **SMART** goal!

FIND AN ACCOUNTABILITY BUDDY

An excellent way to stay focused and productive is to find an accountability buddy. You'll often hear about finding accountability partners when you're pursuing health and fitness goals (going to the gym together or making sure the other person is sticking to their workout routine), but having accountability buddies is a great strategy for any kind of ongoing goal!

Why is external accountability so effective? Think about how many times you've made promises to yourself and broken those promises. Now think about how often you've made promises to other people. Do you have the same track record? Likely not. This is why bringing in someone else to help you with your goals can be so incredibly effective.

Not sure who to invite as your accountability buddy? Here are some ideas:

Family member   *Friend*

Internet friend

Coworker   *Colleague*   *Classmate*

Ultimately, the best accountability buddy is someone you trust who will motivate you to keep you going, even when you don't feel like it. Ask around and find someone this week!

EMBRACE BOREDOM

As you start your journey toward reaching a new goal or becoming an expert at something, it's going to be exciting in the beginning. As it should be! You're starting a new adventure, brimming with motivation and ready to conquer all of the tasks that come with achieving your new goal. However, at some point, boredom will start creeping in and getting comfortable.

No matter how excited you are in the beginning of a project, you're eventually going to get bored. It's these more mundane moments that distinguish those who succeed versus those who throw in the towel. When you're bored, you're more likely to look for distractions, frustrated that what you're working on isn't as interesting anymore. At this stage, you'll need to embrace the boredom. Here are a few ways to do so:

- Avoid distractions as much as possible
- Remember why you started
- Do the boring things first

Stay focused and don't let something new and shiny take you away from doing the hard work. You're on the cusp of something great. Just embrace that boredom and push through to the other side!

JOT DOWN DISTRACTIONS

How often do you get distracted in the middle of working on a project? You're well into finally writing that report you've been putting off for a few days, but then the idea for a brand-new project that you can't wait to get started on suddenly sparks in your head, so you shift your focus. Next thing you know, another hour has gone by and you realize you really need to refocus on that report, but it's hard to bring that momentum back.

Instead of allowing yourself to get distracted with something else, write down your distractions. Literally write down every new idea, desire to pick up your phone, anything that shifts your focus away from what you're currently working on. Use your energy to write it down, so that when you're done with your current priority you can refer back to it later. This way you don't lose your momentum and you have a strategy that supports improving your productivity and focus!

BREAK IT DOWN

Large projects or long-term goals can be intimidating when you're not sure exactly what you should do each day. When you simply include a big project on your to-do list, you're less likely to be productive and more likely to push it off for another day. Break the big project into smaller tasks—as small as you can make them. If you have an upcoming presentation, break it down to what you need to research, the phases of creating your slides, practicing your timing, and so on.

What's a big goal or project that you currently have on your plate? Break it down into small tasks. Put these tasks on your to-do list to increase your productivity and success!

TAKE REGULAR BREAKS

Did you know taking regular breaks will actually help you be *more* productive? Contrary to popular belief, ensuring you're taking time in your day to rest and recalibrate actually helps you stay more productive. When you're not used to taking breaks, it can be hard to get into the habit. Use these steps to get started:

What times of day can you fit at least two 10-minute breaks into your day?

_____

_____

When these times pop up, there's a chance your mind will make excuses about why you shouldn't take a break. Write down three reasons why you need to take these breaks here, and refer back to them whenever you have the urge to skip a break:

_____

_____

_____

_____

_____

_____

_____

_____

_____

REVERSE IT

Using to-do lists as your primary source of reference for productivity is a great tactic to start, but over time if you add too many items to your to-dos every day, you risk a chance of feeling overwhelmed. If you don't finish everything on your list each day, you'll likely feel that you're not doing "enough," when in reality you're doing plenty! If you find yourself feeling this way, try the opposite. Flip your list around, and throughout your day write down everything you've already done. You'll feel so much more accomplished focusing on everything you've finished rather than the items you didn't check off!

Use the space that follows to make your first Already Done List.

_____

_____

_____

_____

_____

_____

_____

_____

_____

_____

_____

REVIEW EACH WEEK

An excellent way to measure how you're working toward achieving your goals is by performing a weekly review. By doing this, you'll be able to see if you need to adjust your approach to anything in order to meet your goals. For example, if you're working toward a healthier lifestyle, and you reflect that you worked out only once this week and ate a lot of sugary foods, then you'll likely conclude that some of these habits need to be adjusted for the following week.

Think about your recent week. What did you accomplish? Did your week's accomplishments help you with your goals?

_____

_____

_____

_____

_____

Is there anything you need to adjust and focus on next week in order to better align with your goals?

_____

_____

_____

_____

CAPTURE THE GOOD SIDE

Technology has given us incredible abilities, such as improving communication, new kinds of careers, and so much more. However, there's another side to technology that's not so great—such as cell phones becoming big sources of distractions. One moment you're fully focused on your task, and the next you're in the black hole of *TikTok*, and 30 minutes of your day have vanished.

What are some positives and negatives that technology has brought into your life?

_____

_____

_____

_____

_____

_____

_____

How can you shift to focus more on utilizing the positives and start to eliminate some of the negative effects of technology?

_____

_____

_____

_____

PART 5

DISCOVER
HOW YOU
Connect with
Others

IDENTIFY YOUR ENERGY

When you think about extroverts and introverts, what's the main difference that comes to mind? Do you associate introverts with being shy and extroverts with being outgoing? While this can be the case, it's not always true. These categories actually describe how a person's energy changes when spending time with other people. Extroverts gain energy when they spend time with others, while introverts lose energy from interactions. If an extrovert spends too much time on their own, they'll start craving connections with other people in order to feel more energized again. If an introvert spends too much time socializing, they'll start needing time alone to recharge.

Do you know if you're an introvert or extrovert? If you're not sure, pay attention to how you feel the next time you're with a group of people. How's your energy? Are you buzzing and feeling good after hours of spending time with others? Or do you feel like you need some time to relax? Understanding this aspect of your character can help you better understand other facets of your life, especially when it comes to relationships with other people.

ESTABLISH HEALTHY BOUNDARIES

Healthy boundaries are incredibly important for all of the relationships in your life. In addition to enhancing relationships, boundaries help improve your self-esteem, protect your emotional energy, and help you gain more independence. How are the boundaries in your life?

Take some time to reflect on some of your closest relationships. List the people you are closest to here:

_____

_____

_____

_____

Reflect on how you typically interact with each person in this list. Notice if you ever feel especially drained or energetically low after interacting with any of these people. If this is the case, you likely need stronger boundaries. To do this, reflect on the values you identified earlier in this book and what you need out of relationships. Do any of these values or needs feel compromised by the people on this list? If so, write those here:

_____

_____

_____

_____

_____

_____

Now decide on which boundaries you need to establish in order to uphold those important values and needs. Some examples of boundaries include scheduling time for yourself and sticking to it, saying no when you want to, and not allowing other people to talk to you in ways that make you feel uncomfortable. Write your boundaries here:

Once you decide on the boundaries you need, communicate them to others. Be clear, firm, and fair. They may feel uncomfortable, but in the end the people who truly care about you will grow to understand that honoring your boundaries is important to having the best relationship possible with you, and that in turn will help you be the best version of yourself.

REFLECT ON YOUR FRIENDSHIPS

How are your friendships? Are they mostly positive, or do you have a few friends who bring more drama into your life than others? Take some time to think about these important people in your life, and be honest with yourself. You deserve to give your energy and love to friends who care about you and have your best interest at heart. If you have any friendships that don't operate this way, think about whether you need to have a discussion with this person or even reevaluate the friendship all together. Note these thoughts here.

DESCRIBE YOUR IDEAL PARTNER

If you would like to get married one day but have yet to find the right person to take that big step with, a great place to start is by identifying what important qualities and values you're looking for in an ideal partner. No individual is perfect, but you may have specific nonnegotiables in mind (like wanting to have a family, sharing the same values, etc.). Describe what this ideal partner would look like for you in the following space. If these are all truly things that you aren't willing to compromise in a partner, keep them close to your heart as you start meeting new people.

IDENTIFY POSITIVE RELATIONSHIPS

Who are the people who have created a positive impact in your life?
Think back even to when you were a kid. Are there any relatives,
teachers, friends, or coaches who pushed you to be the person you
are today? Name a few people who come to mind.

_____

_____

_____

_____

_____

_____

_____

Is there anything that all of these people have in common? If so,
keep an eye out for people who share similar characteristics, and
take a moment to feel gratitude for the privilege that you've been
able to have such wonderful people in your life!

_____

_____

_____

_____

DESCRIBE YOUR ROLE MODELS

Who are the people you look up to? Are they people you know personally or figures from history? Write a list of them here. Leave a little bit of space next to each name, and use that space to identify one quality that you admire in each of these role models.

_____

_____

_____

_____

_____

_____

_____

_____

_____

_____

_____

_____

In what ways can you bring some of these qualities into your own life? If these individuals are people you admire, why not become a similar role model for yourself?

APPRECIATE YOUR BIGGEST FANS

Who are the people in your life who have supported you the most? Whether you've been working toward big dreams or experiencing some tough moments, who are the people who always believe in you? These people are your biggest fans. They love and care about you so much that they want nothing but the best for you—and believe you can achieve anything! If you know even one person like this in your life, you're incredibly blessed. Even one single supporter can really make a positive difference when it comes to pushing through the hard days. (And if you can't think of anyone, how about yourself? You can be your own biggest cheerleader!)

When was the last time you expressed appreciation to the biggest fans in your life? Take some time this week to share gratitude to your supporters. Even a simple note saying,

can go a long way. You could write a letter, make a phone call, or send them a card or a meaningful text. Expressing this appreciation will not only help them feel good, but make you feel good as well!

BRING DOWN THE WALLS

If you've experienced betrayals from previous friends, have dealt with a compulsive liar, or simply have been frequently disappointed by other people, building trust can be a challenging task. However, even though it can be difficult, trust is absolutely essential for building healthy, long-lasting relationships, whether romantic or otherwise.

If you struggle with trusting other people, start small. You don't need to suddenly start expecting that everyone will have your back. Instead, pick one person who you're becoming comfortable with, and tell them one simple thing about yourself. Alternatively, you can ask someone for a small favor and see how they respond. Bit by bit, each small moment and opportunity can build deeper trust until you have built a strong foundation in a relationship you may have never thought possible! Be patient as you go through these baby steps: It's a process that takes time. And that's okay! Trust is so valuable that the extra time, patience, and effort are worth it when you've developed an invaluable connection with someone else.

BLOCK OUT OTHER PEOPLE'S OPINIONS

How many times have you found yourself holding back from being fully yourself because you're scared of what other people will think about you? Maybe you didn't speak up in a meeting at work because you were afraid one of your coworkers would judge you. Maybe you've held back from suggesting what to do for fun with friends because you weren't sure if they would agree.

If you relate to this, how much do you think other people's opinions have been holding you back from living your fullest, most authentic life?

Here's the thing: Other people's opinions don't matter. They really don't. Sure, you may respect someone's advice or appreciate insight on something in your life, but at the end of the day you need to choose whatever feels right for *you*. Everyone's opinions are based on their own life experiences and values, which are always going to be different from your own.

Next time you find yourself holding back in fear of someone else's opinion, ask yourself these three questions:

1. What do I think?

2. Why do I care about this person's opinion?

3. Does their opinion really matter?

After you answer these questions, you should be able to filter through what *you* actually want, rather than depending on what other people think. Changing this specific habit will unlock so many amazing opportunities in your life!

RESOLVE CONFLICTS

Dealing with conflict is always a challenging situation, but how do you handle it? Are you usually more shy and passive, or are you straight and to the point with other people? Whether you're one of these two types or somewhere in between, the key to handling conflict or confrontation successfully is open and honest conversation (from *both* sides). With this in mind, how can you improve your conflict communication efforts with other people? For example, if you're a headstrong type, maybe you can practice listening better to the other person's point of view. If you're a passive type, maybe you can more actively stand up for your own values. Explore your options in the following space, and keep these ideas in mind the next time you experience conflict with someone else.

STOP PEOPLE PLEASING

People pleasers constantly strive to make other people happy. While the intention may sound noble, people pleasers usually ignore their own needs in order to put other people first. Along with this tendency, other people-pleasing behaviors include saying yes to everyone's requests, constantly apologizing, taking on an overwhelming number of responsibilities, and being terrified of disappointing other people.

Does this sound like you? If so, there are ways you can start recovering from these people-pleasing habits and put yourself first instead. Try these changes:

- ✔ Identify your own needs and values
- ✔ Start actually saying no when you don't want to do something
- ✔ Set healthy boundaries with other people

While this isn't an exhaustive list, these are some of the first steps you can take to break your people-pleasing habits and start living your life for you rather than for other people.

DISCOVER YOUR LOVE LANGUAGE

Do you know your love language? According to the book *The 5 Love Languages* by Gary Chapman, love languages are how you prefer to both give and receive love. The five different types are:

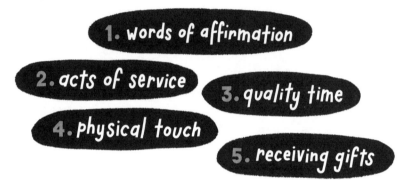

1. words of affirmation
2. acts of service
3. quality time
4. physical touch
5. receiving gifts

While everyone may enjoy both giving and receiving love in many of these different ways, you will have a natural preference for one love language over the others. Once you understand your love language, you can use this new understanding to connect with other people and relationships in your life (both romantic and platonic).

Go to www.5lovelanguages.com and take the quick quiz to learn about your top love language. Once you learn yours and read more about the others, notice how the people in your life respond to these ways of giving and receiving love. If you know someone else's love language, start to use their preferred love language with the intention of strengthening your relationship. Additionally, communicate your love language and needs with others in your life, so they have a better understanding of how they can express their appreciation to you in the best way possible.

START SAYING NO

Saying no to other people is tough if you're used to constantly saying yes because you want to make other people happy. However, if you're saying yes so often that you're overflowing with responsibilities for other people and have no time for yourself, then you need to start rethinking your approach!

Saying no doesn't have to be hard; it's simply a way to enforce healthy boundaries to help protect your own time, energy, and mental health. If you're not sure how to say no to other people, here are a couple ways you can start:

> " *I need to check my schedule, let me get back to you.* "

> " *Thank you, I appreciate the offer, but not at this time.* "

Work your way up to a simple no as you get more comfortable with less direct versions. You don't owe an explanation or an apology to anyone. It can be uncomfortable at first, but it gets easier over time with more practice!

FOCUS ON YOU

Did you know that sometimes the best thing you can do for your relationships is to focus on yourself by making your self-care and self-worth a top priority? When you work on yourself, you have the ability to learn more about who you are, what areas need the most attention, and how you can be a better friend, partner, and so on to other people.

The good news? You're reading this book: That's a huge step! Now let's take another step. What's one thing that you can do this week that makes you feel good?

_____

_____

_____

_____

_____

_____

Take time this week for at least three days to do this activity. Schedule it, set an alarm—do anything you need to make it a priority. Notice how you feel after only three days, and imagine how you'll feel after incorporating it into your life on a regular basis!

EMBRACE THE PUSH AND PULL

Some people will always be put off or pushed away by some aspect of your personality. For example, someone might see your outgoing, fun nature as "too loud" or "aggressive" for them and not feel inclined to further a friendship with you. The most important thing to remember from situations like this is that it's 100 percent the other person's decision, and it's ultimately their loss. Because the people in your life who care about and love you will love every part of you, including these things that seemingly "push" other people away.

What are some qualities about yourself that you feel sometimes push some people away?

_____

_____

_____

_____

_____

Alternatively, how do these same characteristics pull you closer to the important people in your life?

_____

_____

_____

_____

_____

ASK FOR HELP

Are you someone who has a hard time asking for help from other people? No matter what you believe, asking someone for help when you genuinely need it is not a sign of weakness. In fact, asking someone to assist you with something will not only help you learn something new and feel less stressed, but it can also enable you to build a stronger relationship with that person. Asking for help tells the other person that you trust their knowledge and experience.

For example, if you're at work and your workload is overflowing with too much to do, asking a coworker to help you with some of your projects shows that you trust them to help you with your job. Additionally, they may have a new way of working through a project or tricky situation that you hadn't thought of before. Likewise, you probably have something new that you could teach them!

There are so many positive opportunities that can happen when you start allowing yourself to ask other people for help. Don't ever feel guilty or shameful for doing so—you're not meant to do everything on your own.

BE THE PARTNER YOU WOULD WANT

Often when you're thinking about your ideal relationship with a future partner, you default to thinking about what qualities you're looking for in the other person. While it's definitely a good idea to know what qualities and values are important to you in a partner, have you thought about what *you* bring into your relationships?

Flip the script: What are the best qualities that you will bring to your future ideal relationship? Are you a good listener? Family oriented? Do you value honesty and integrity? Write down these qualities here:

_____

_____

_____

_____

_____

_____

_____

_____

_____

Keep these qualities in mind when you're meeting new people and exploring new relationships. If your confidence starts to falter, know that you bring all of these incredible values and qualities to both your relationship with someone else and the relationship you have with yourself.

NOTICE THE PATTERNS

Have you experienced a series of negative relationships or friendships in your life? When was the last time you reflected on what happened to sour them? Maybe you and a friend had a falling-out over lack of respect for your boundaries, or you and a partner split due to poor communication. When you look back, you may notice some patterns that happened within each of these more negative experiences with previous friends and/or partners.

Take some time to really reflect on some of your previous relationships.

Are there any common issues or situations that pop up with multiple people?

_____

_____

_____

_____

_____

What lessons can you learn from these recurring patterns?

_____

_____

_____

_____

_____

BALANCE YOUR TRUE SELF

Have you ever noticed that you have a different persona depending on who you're spending time with? For example, maybe you're a slightly different person when you're around your coworkers compared to how you act around your closest friends. While it's okay to an extent to have a different approach depending on the relationship (you normally need a more professional persona at work versus with your family), it's important to make sure that at the end of the day you're still staying true to yourself.

How do you ensure that you're staying authentic to who you really are? Pay attention to how you feel when you're around other people. Notice if what you're saying or doing feels out of alignment for you. Do you feel like you're pretending to be something that you're not? If you notice yourself acting this way around certain people, think about how you can adjust your behavior to better fit your true self. When you make decisions, remember your core values and what's important to you. As long as you're embodying those, you're well on your way to being your most authentic version of yourself around anyone.

UNHOOK FROM PRAISE

If you're truly going to start putting yourself first, stop people pleasing, and really understand who you are and what you want in life, you need to stop relying on praise and approval from other people. Why? Because you're probably doing the following:

- ✔ Making choices based on the opinions of other people

- ✔ Feeling terrified of criticism and going out of your own way to make sure you never hear anything negative from those around you

- ✔ Self-sabotaging—ruining your goals due to the fear of what other people will think or past negative feedback

The reality? Opinions—even the good ones—are subjective. Praise and criticism are more a reflection of the person giving feedback than of you or your work. Think about movie reviews: Some critics *rave* about certain movies, but you might hate the same film. Does that make the film "good" or "bad"? It depends on the person and their own preferences.

It's up to *you*, not other people, to create your own fulfillment. Next time you notice yourself making decisions or seeking praise from someone else, turn inward and ask yourself how *you* feel about what you're doing. If you like it and think it's good enough, then that's all you need!

GET OUT OF THE COMPARISON TRAP

Getting stuck in the comparison trap is a slippery slope. Not only is comparing yourself to other people detrimental for your confidence level and damaging for your relationships, but it can cause unnecessary anxiety and stress. Next time you find yourself negatively comparing your life and progress to other people—whether those you know in real life or those you follow on social media—try these steps:

1 **PUT YOURSELF IN THEIR SHOES:**
When you see someone else's successes and happy moments on social media, do you really think you're seeing the full story? Consider what challenges other people may have experienced in order to achieve their success. No one is immune to difficult situations, no matter how successful they look online.

2 **FLIP THE SCRIPT:**
Pretend you're someone else comparing themselves to you. What do you think other people are jealous of when they look at your social media profiles or meet you in real life and see your successes? You may be surprised just how much progress you're making when you change your perspective.

It takes practice, but trying these steps and focusing on the positive aspects of your relationships with others rather than comparing yourselves to them will help you finally break free from the comparison trap and create stronger bonds in the process.

NAVIGATE JEALOUSY

Jealousy—the green-eyed monster that gets the best of all of us every now and then. It's a natural human emotion, rooted in the basis of comparing yourself to someone else as well as your own insecurities. Whether you struggle with jealousy in your romantic relationship or when seeing someone else living your dream life, you don't have to let jealousy take hold of your life. There are ways of navigating jealousy to calm this little monster and guide your emotions toward gratitude and love.

Are you feeling jealous of someone right now?
What are the thoughts that pop up?

_____

_____

_____

What do you think is the root cause of this jealousy?
(E.g., You're jealous of someone else's relationship because
you haven't had luck with dating.)

_____

_____

How can you turn your attention inward and serve this need?
(E.g., Keep meeting new people with an open mind,
if that's what you want!)

_____

_____

TAKE YOURSELF OUT

Whether you're currently single or in a relationship, the relationship you develop with yourself is just as important as the one you have with someone else. In fact, the more you understand and accept all parts of yourself, the more you'll understand how you can be the best partner or friend to someone else in a way that works best for the both of you. One way to get to know yourself better? Take yourself out on a date!

Why wait around for another person to go try new things or experience restaurants you love? Do it for you! If you've never taken a solo date before, you might feel a little uncomfortable at first. That's okay: It's a new experience, and it'll feel more comfortable the more you try it. Not sure where to start? Here are some ideas you can try this week to take yourself out on a solo date:

- ✔ Spend some time at your favorite coffee shop
- ✔ Try a new restaurant you've discovered
- ✔ Go for a walk in the park
- ✔ Take a class to learn a new skill (cooking, dance, photography, anything!)
- ✔ Explore a local museum
- ✔ Try one activity on your bucket list
- ✔ Take a quick road trip to a nearby city you've wanted to explore

BRING YOUR VISION TO LIFE

Earlier in Part 5, you took time to describe your ideal partner. If you're someone who currently wants a partner, think about all of the places and activities that you would like to experience when you're in a relationship. Where would you go? What would you do together? You may have identified this in the previous journal exercise, but if not, picture it in your head right now. Now bring that vision to life! Go participate in these activities and explore these places. Why not open up your chances to finding someone who's already participating in these activities that you enjoy?

Let's say you would love to find someone who has the same passion for rock climbing as you. Join a climbing group or a gym! If you already regularly participate in climbing, keep an open mind and heart with the people that you meet. Take it outside of the gym and invite someone to lunch. You never know who you'll form a connection with, even as a friend!

TUNE IN TO BODY LANGUAGE

Learning how to effectively communicate with other people is extremely important, and a key piece of communication is body language. It may take practice to recognize what someone's body language means, but the way they're positioning themselves could tell you a lot about how they're actually feeling versus what they're telling you.

While there are many ways you can interpret body language, the two basic categories that you can start focusing on are open and closed positions. If someone has good posture, solid eye contact, and an overall relaxed disposition, they have a more open body position. This means that they're listening and likely will have a more positive response to your conversation. If someone has poor posture, avoids eye contact, and is crossing their arms, they have a more closed body position. This can mean that they're uncomfortable and likely not open to what you're discussing at that time.

Keep an eye on these nonverbal cues when you're having important conversations. They may shed light on how you need to switch your approach to your conversation, or let you know that the conversation is productive. Pay attention to your body language too! You may be sending them more cues than you think.

DISCOVER MORE TOGETHER

If you're currently in a relationship, you're likely learning a lot about yourself every day. Being with someone else opens you up to new opportunities of self-discovery in ways that you may not have been able to explore when you were single. This isn't to say that you can only fully explore your self-discovery journey if you're with someone else; it's simply a different way you can continue your journey. For example, if you're living with your significant other, you're likely learning new things about yourself in regard to living styles and communication with other people.

What have you learned about yourself throughout your relationship so far?

GROW FROM THE HEARTBREAK

Breakups are tough. Whether you're the one making the decision or the other person has made it for you, you will have challenging emotions to navigate. Over time as you heal, you'll notice that you can learn a lot about yourself during this challenging experience. You'll learn what you're actually looking for in a relationship, what you need from a partner, how you heal through heartbreak, and so much more.

> If you've experienced a breakup in the past, what did you learn about yourself and what you want and need in the process?

STRENGTHEN YOUR RELATIONSHIPS

Is there someone in your life who you care about deeply but who you've been drifting away from, whether it's a friend, relative, or romantic partner? Strengthening existing relationships with other people is important, even if they're people who have been in your life for a long time. Making the extra effort to strengthen the bond with another person in your life will help you both grow and appreciate each other even more in the long run.

Not sure how to take steps toward strengthening your relationships with other important people in your life? Try one of these this week:

- ✔ Invite them out to eat or for coffee, and don't let your phone distract you from the conversation.

- ✔ Ask them questions. Learn even more about them that you didn't know before.

- ✔ Send them handwritten letters, expressing your gratitude for having them in your life.

- ✔ Call them instead of texting. Hearing someone's voice can have a big impact in a conversation.

- ✔ Plan a trip together, even a short day trip exploring something new.

FACE YOUR FEARS

Meeting new people can be a scary experience, especially when it comes to meeting new potential romantic partners. When you've had bad relationships in the past, fear is likely holding you back from taking risks and meeting new people, even if it's something you truly want to do.

The good news? What you've experienced in your past, you've overcome. You're here now and can handle more than you think.

What scares you when it comes to exploring new relationships?

_____

_____

_____

In what ways have you overcome these fears and experiences in the past?

_____

_____

_____

How will you handle these experiences if you face them in the future?

_____

_____

_____

You are incredibly capable. If finding a new relationship is something you truly want for yourself, don't let these fears hold you back from taking the chance at finding someone special.

ABOUT THE AUTHOR

SARA KATHERINE is a self-discovery coach, podcast host for *Be Your Own Badass*, and the author of *I'm Awesome. Here's Why...* and *Be Happy. Be Calm. Be YOU*. After publishing her first book, *Sara Earns Her Ears*, she launched her current self-discovery coaching business at Sara-Katherine.com, where she strives to help empower others to understand who they are and what they want in order to confidently live their best lives. Born and raised in California, Sara also loves Disney, Marvel movies, and her cats, Mochi and Brie.